Aquarius

The Ultimate Guide to an Amazing Zodiac Sign in Astrology

© Copyright 2020

The contents of this book may not be reproduced, duplicated, or transmitted without direct written permission from the author.

Under no circumstances will any legal responsibility or blame be held against the publisher for any reparation, damages, or monetary loss due to the information herein, either directly or indirectly.

Legal Notice: This book is copyright protected. This is only for personal use. You cannot amend, distribute, sell, use, quote, or paraphrase any part of the content within this book without the consent of the author.

Disclaimer Notice: Please note the information within this document is for educational and entertainment purposes only. Every attempt has been made to provide accurate, up to date, and reliable complete information. No warranties of any kind are expressed or implied. Readers acknowledge that the author is not engaging in the rendering of legal, financial, medical, or professional advice. The content of this book has been derived from various sources. Please consult a licensed professional before attempting any techniques outlined in this book.

By reading this document, the reader agrees that under no circumstances is the author responsible for any losses, direct or indirect, which are incurred as a result of the use of information within this document, including, but not limited to, errors, omissions, or inaccuracies.

Your Free Gift (only available for a limited time)

Thanks for getting this book! If you want to learn more about various spirituality topics, then join Mari Silva's community and get a free guided meditation MP3 for awakening your third eye. This guided meditation mp3 is designed to open and strengthen ones third eye so you can experience a higher state of consciousness. Simply visit the link below the image to get started.

https://spiritualityspot.com/meditation

Contents

INTRODUCTION 1

CHAPTER ONE: AN INTRODUCTION TO AQUARIUS 3
- The Aquarius Myth 3
- The Aquarius Glyph and Its Meaning 5
- The Aquarius Planets 7
- House of Aquarius 8
- Eleventh House 8
- Colors for Aquarius 9
- Birthstone for Aquarius 10
- Other Lucky Stones for the Aquarius 10
- Lucky Stone for Aquarius Woman 11
- Lucky Stone for Aquarius Man 11
- Characteristics of Aquarius 12
- Positive Aquarius Traits 12
- Negative Aquarius Traits 14
- Aquarius Characteristics in Common Situations 15
- Aquarius Celebrities Who Espouse the Traits of the Sign 17

CHAPTER TWO: AQUARIUS STRENGTHS AND WEAKNESSES ... 20
- Positive Traits 20
- Aquarius Negative Traits 24
- The Aquarius Woman: Key Traits 26
- The Aquarius Man: Key Traits 31

CHAPTER THREE: CUSPS 37
- Cusp and Its Effects 38
- Capricorn-Aquarius Cusp Character Traits 40
- Aquarius-Pisces Personality Traits 46

CHAPTER FOUR: THE AQUARIUS CHILD 52

Differences Between Aquarius Girls and Boys 58
Things That You Need To Know About an Aquarian Child 59
What to Expect When Raising an Aquarian Child 63
Tips and Tricks 65
All About the Aquarius Teenager 67
Aquarius Teen's Likes 68
An Aquarius Teen's Dislikes 69

CHAPTER FIVE: AQUARIUS AND FRIENDSHIP 70

Aquarians As Friends 70
Aquarius and Friendship 72
Aquarians at a Party 76
Tips On How to be Friends with Aquarians 78

CHAPTER SIX: AQUARIUS IN LOVE 81

CHAPTER SEVEN: AQUARIUS AT WORK 91

Careers Options for Aquarius Individuals 92
Aquarius in the Workplace 95
Workplace Compatibility with other Zodiac Signs 96

CONCLUSION 103

HERE'S ANOTHER BOOK BY MARI SILVA THAT YOU MIGHT LIKE 104

YOUR FREE GIFT (ONLY AVAILABLE FOR A LIMITED TIME) 105

REFERENCES 106

Introduction

People have been fascinated with the stars and the planets since ancient times. Before technology and the Internet became prevalent, the stars and planets acted as a guide to life and to the future. In the olden days, we had a much stronger connection with the celestial realm and the earth under our feet. Ancient stories and myths surround these celestial bodies, but the world we live in now is quite different.

Science is considered the real truth and everything else is questioned, but there is a little truth in everything, and this applies to the ancient art of astrology. Believing in zodiac signs and their relevance in our lives is something that many people have been opening up to again. It is not necessary to believe only in what you see or what is proven by science. You can also choose to believe in things that are beyond your understanding. This is why I encourage the exploration of zodiac signs.

Depending on the season and the day you were born, you will fall under one of the twelve zodiac signs. Learning about your own zodiac sign or that of the people around you can be immensely helpful. Most people know their zodiac sign, and a lot of them read their horoscope quite often as well.

In this book, we will specifically focus on Aquarius and endeavor to give you an in-depth understanding of any individual who belongs to this sign.

This book highlights the strengths, weaknesses, unique traits, and quirks of Aquarians. It will also give you a better idea about the compatibility in love, work, and friendship of an Aquarius individual with all the other signs.

The things you learn in this book might surprise you as you realize how much of it resonates with you or the Aquarius in your life. Essentially, this book should help any Aquarius understand themselves better, gain a better balance in life, and learn a lot about how great the impact of their zodiac sign is on their lives.

If you are ready to delve into the world of Aquarius, start reading!

Chapter One: An Introduction to Aquarius

Aquarius is one of the fascinating signs of the zodiac and is often considered "the alien sign." It is a quirky, unique, and a sometimes-bizarre sign that is full of heart and love. This chapter will help you understand the intricate details of this sign.

The astrological sign Aquarius appears eleventh in the Zodiac. It is a representation of the Aquarius constellation. The Sun enters this sign around January 21 and leaves on February 20 in the tropical zodiac. In the sidereal zodiac, the Sun enters this sign on February 15 and leaves on March 14. This factor is also affected by the leap year phenomenon.

The Aquarius Myth

The zodiac constellation of Aquarius is represented as a water bearer. This water bearer was Ganymede, a Phrygian youth from Greek mythology. He was the son of King Tros, the ruler of Troy. According to other sources, he may have been the son of Dardanus. One day Ganymede was tending the flock of sheep for his father when Zeus saw him and lost his heart to him. He assumed the form of a huge bird and bundled Ganymede away. From then on, Ganymede became the cupbearer of the gods. Orpheus sings this tale in the works of Ovid.

Constellation

The Aquarius constellation is a winter constellation situated next to Cetus and Pisces in the northern hemisphere. It is a fairly radiant constellation.

Symbol for Aquarius

As mentioned, Aquarius is usually represented as a water-bearer. This symbol is often depicted in other forms, such as a wise man, a young woman, or an old person. Sometimes only a pot filled with water is used to represent the sign. (The representation is merely conceptual and not a perfect definition of the sign.)

There are many ways for the symbol of Aquarius to be interpreted. For instance, one interpretation says that the collection of water represents the collection of wisdom. The Aquarius individual or soul is always in search of wisdom and is the bearer of the collective wisdom of humankind. It may sound quite lofty, but people who know Aquarian individuals will agree that this makes sense on a deep level.

Aquarian individuals believe in the essence of life and have tremendous healing capacity. They love to better their surroundings and community and perform acts of altruism. They like to improve the lives of people around them. They do these acts because they enjoy it, not for praise or credit. Aquarius dispenses kindness, wisdom, and serendipity through his pot.

In ancient times, the water bearer would walk many miles just to fetch fresh water for their community. Similarly, the Aquarius person is ready to travel through pain, difficulties, and struggle to search for truth, enlightening ideas, and wisdom. They would gladly walk the paths that others avoid.

The Aquarius Glyph and Its Meaning

To describe the zodiac signs in shorthand, astrologers all over the world use specific glyphs and signs. These are unique and different for each star sign and hold crucial meaning in representing the sign. The glyphs are simple, so anyone can emulate them with ease. The glyph for Aquarius, too, is simple, but it encompasses a deep meaning and represents the sign in the best way possible.

Many people get the Aquarius symbol as a tattoo. It is represented using choppy waters or a bolt of lightning. The choppy-waters glyph has two waves moving in parallel. This glyph showcases the deep hidden nature of the sign.

Aquarius is an intelligent sign blessed with the power of intuition. This allows them to know things, even if they do not understand the reason. The parallel-wave lines also depict an Aquarian desire for equality. You can notice these factors in any typical Aquarian person. They hate the disparity between classes, gender, etc. For them, everyone is equal. They have the desire to make and see the world in an equal light.

They believe that this can be done by bringing the great truths to light so that humankind can benefit from them. They are aware of the fact that this act can isolate or alienate them, but they gladly walk this difficult path with immense bravery.

Element

Each zodiac sign is ruled by one of the four elements: air, water, earth, or fire. The zodiac signs form four trios; therefore, you can see the overlapping of emotions, traits, and actions in signs belonging to the same trio.

Many beginners are often surprised to realize that the element of water does not rule Aquarius. The glyph has waves; the symbol of Aquarius is a water bearer; all these factors would seem to indicate that the sign has a close relationship with water, but it is governed by air.

Aquarians hate conventions and will never bow down to anyone's expectations; it is no wonder their ruling element shatters the expectations in this matter. The Air trio is comprised of Gemini, Aquarius, and Libra. All of these signs have a fast-moving outlook on life. They are witty, sharp, and intellectual. While the signs are similar in certain ways, Aquarius differs from the others because of particular characteristics.

The element of Air in the zodiac stands for ideas, thoughts, and intellectual reasoning. Aquarian individuals are often confused because they love humanity but do not understand emotions and feelings. This creates a constant sense of confusion. They are often unlucky in love, though it's no fault of theirs. As an Aquarian, the biggest issue that you may have to face is the difficult nature of heavy emotions such as sorrow, love, and grief.

Emotions such as these become immensely complicated when you try to approach them from an intellectual point of view, as would an Aquarius. When Aquarians do not have their reason to rely on, they get confused and frightened by their feelings. It is necessary to maintain your composure while dealing with a person of this sign.

These individuals often have profound and grand ideas, while eschewing shallow thoughts. They are artistic, distinct, and bold. They are provocative and enjoy humanity, and they help people with their combination of intuition and intelligence.

The heads of Aquarian individuals are full of ideas that move through their brains swiftly. They talk with passion and vividness. The sheer number of ideas often drives them in circles and throws them off towards tangential topics. As a friend of an Aquarius, be patient when they do this. Their mind moves in all directions with the speed of light. If they do not come back to the topic soon, you can nudge them in the right direction.

The Aquarius Planets

Each zodiac sign has particular elements or items that represent them. These include glyphs, symbols, elements, constellations, etc. Another factor that rules the zodiac signs is their planet; a particular "astrological planet", which generally correlates to one of the physical planets in our solar system, rules each sign.

According to astronomy, there are eight planets in the solar system, but in astrology there are more than eight. Some signs also share planets. Thanks to modern science, new planets have been discovered; over time, that has led to changes in the classical list of ruling planets. For instance, Mars once ruled the sign Scorpio, but Pluto (which incidentally is no longer a planet) rules it now. Certain other bodies of the Solar System also govern some zodiac signs; for instance, the Moon governs Cancer.

In the case of Aquarius, both Saturn and Uranus govern it. The interpretations of the traits and effects of both these planets differ a lot, but both work in tandem to bring the uniqueness of their personality to the forefront.

Saturn is a stern planet in the solar system, according to most interpretations. It is focused on self-discipline, order, and method. A code of conduct still governs even the most outlandish Aquarius people. This code of conduct is often personal and does not follow the code of conduct of other people.

Uranus is a planet that loves to do things of its own accord, just like the Aquarius individual who is unique and bold. Uranus rules higher learning, wisdom, new possibilities, freedom, and a passion for change. These traits are quite typical of the Aquarius person.

People are often scared and nervous about big changes, but Aquarius accepts them gladly and often enjoys them. They believe that life should always move forward, albeit in harmony and peace.

They are full of wisdom and lofty ideals presented with total compassion.

House of Aquarius

Astrology is an infinite field, and a multitude of factors make it an intricate art. Even at the most basic level, there exists a lot of different concepts that make it difficult to understand for a beginner. For instance, along with the twelve zodiac signs, there are twelve houses. If you do not understand houses, you have most likely skipped over an integral aspect of astrology.

Astrological houses stand for the exact areas of a person's life that the horoscope talks about. Each house in astrology represents a unique factor. These houses stand for the places, people, situations, and circumstances that take place in life.

Each house is named after the zodiac signs, so they begin at Aries and end with Pisces. Each house has a particular feature, according to the zodiac wheel. To interpret the houses, you need to have a birth chart.

Eleventh House

The Eleventh House is the house of Aquarius. It is where you make your debut in society. It also stands for the reception or reaction that you get from society. It is considered to be the house of friends. It also includes other social circles such as colleagues and acquaintances. Like the sign, this house, too, is ruled by both Saturn and Uranus.

The Eleventh house shows whether you fit in or break away from your birth conditions and how you were raised. It sets the mood for these factors.

A person with a strong Eleventh House often ends in a tribe totally different from where he was born. Their original tribe may make them feel like an alien or an outsider. Other strong Eleventh House individuals may provoke the people around them and may break the traditions in which they were raised.

The ruler of this house is Saturn, along with Uranus. This house represents community, expression of the community, shared visions, collaborations, and togetherness.

House of Good Spirit

The ancient Greek astrologers looked at the Eleventh House as the house of aspirations. It is considered the house of good spirit and freedom, as it feels free after breaking the conventions of the society with no care for those involved. This provides its spaciousness that harkens to the guiding element of air. It allows it to be dreamy without any judgment.

The house is also known as the House of Divinity and is full of compassion. It allows the person to have a total big picture of humanity.

Many astrologers find it difficult or tricky to define the house, as it is full of contradictions, just like the sign itself. Both aspects allow for the simultaneous yet contradictory implications of individual aspirations, along with the potency of a group.

Colors for Aquarius

Aquarians are often considered the aliens of the zodiac system, as they are unique, think outside the box, and are way ahead of their time. They tend to look at the bigger picture and are thorough humanitarians. They strive hard to make the world a better place. They are often considered weird or slightly eccentric, but these factors make them even more endearing. This is why Aquarians have a lot of friends from various walks of life. This section will help you understand which colors are the best for Aquarians.

While Aquarius people dress and act in a way that makes them stand apart, there are certain colors that are genuinely good for the sign. Every zodiac sign has certain colors that are "suitable" for them.

Blue: a water bearer represents Aquarius, and not surprisingly, the power color for the sign is blue. Aquarians, like the water bearer, bear and bring knowledge and wisdom to the world. The color blue keeps them centered and calm. As Aquarians have the habit of going off tangents, the color blue can keep them grounded. It provides a calming aura that can keep them stable and focused.

Another color highly recommended for Aquarius is purple. The gemstone of Aquarius is amethyst, a bright purple crystal. It is a psychic stone that can enhance the wearer's intuition and other "psychic" abilities. Amethyst represents wisdom, compassion, and idealism, which are important traits of Aquarius. The overall persona of this sign is of intelligence and compassion.

Birthstone for Aquarius

According to astrology, Saturn is considered the toughest planet. This planet (along with Uranus) is supposed to rule Aquarius. Any Aquarian who can satisfy Saturn and make the planet happy will be a huge success in almost all walks of life. The favorite stone of this planet is Blue Sapphire. This is why Blue Sapphire is considered the birthstone of Aquarians. It is recommended to wear this stone on the middle finger in a ring made of gold. Wearing this on the right hand will improve the overall quality of your life.

Other Lucky Stones for the Aquarius

There are many other stones that are considered lucky and powerful for Aquarius. Some of these include garnet, amber, amethyst, opal, moss agate, sugilite, etc. The talismanic stone of Aquarius is jasper, while its planetary stone is turquoise. Let us have a look at this subject of stones, one by one.

Amber Stone

It is good for keeping negative energy at bay.

Amethyst

It is a healing stone that can help you get rid of past sorrows and guilt.

Garnet

It is another health stone that can help you achieve good health.

Hematite

It is a calming stone that takes away negative energy, pressure, and stress. It is good for self-confidence. It acts upon the Root Chakra and can convert the negative energy into positive vibrations.

Lucky Stone for Aquarius Woman

For Aquarian women, the following are the best stones:

- Agate
- Turquoise
- Garnet
- Amethyst

Lucky Stone for Aquarius Man

Aquarian men should wear these gems to bring about positive changes in their life:

- Jasper
- Garnet
- Amethyst

It is necessary to choose the right gemstone associated with your zodiac sign. If you choose an incorrect one, it may lead to the development of a variety of problems.

Characteristics of Aquarius

Aquarius individuals are generous and give with open hands, but they often get lost in their plans, ideas, questions, and creative solutions. They generally despise people breaking in on their thought process, but if you see an Aquarius friend being too lofty, it is your duty to bring them back to reality; otherwise, they might get too lost in thought.

It is also necessary to remember that, with their uniqueness, they are blessed with remarkable and powerful insight. Under their outlandish and sometimes strange outer appearance, they hide a pioneering approach towards the world, which can lead us all forward.

Aquarians have a set of characteristics found in most individuals belonging to this sign. These characteristics are positive ones as well as negative ones. It is recommended to enhance the positive characteristics and get rid of the negative ones to make your life more enjoyable.

Positive Aquarius Traits

Aquarians are often described as original, intelligent, and smart. They are future-oriented and are the visionaries of this world. Some of their positive traits are:

Vision

The most common and prominent trait of this sign is ambition and vision. They are highly ambitious about their personal and social future. Thanks to their humanitarian nature, Aquarians care for society's betterment and will put in a lot of effort to lead society towards a glorious future. They undertake various generous humanitarian causes such as fighting against world hunger, finding new ways to stop climate change, and tackling poverty and corruption.

Aquarians can be slightly dogmatic in their beliefs sometimes, but they will often do whatever they can do to make the world a better place. They have a strong sense of justice and compassion. A combination of both guides their views and actions. They enjoy and love freedom and extend it to everyone.

Aquarians can change the world with their passion, humanitarian will, and unique perspectives.

Intelligent

One of the most cerebral signs, Aquarians tend to be highly intelligent but often get lost in analyzing things to find new solutions to a problem. Their intelligence is not limited to books alone, and it is possible to find Aquarians who are experts in various fields. They see possibilities in almost everything and love to analyze and dissect things. This makes them highly tolerant of a variety of viewpoints.

Aquarians tend to look at the big-picture, which makes them highly suited to solving problems. Their own ideas and constant bombardment of thoughts may distract them, but if and when focused, they can produce the best suggestions and well-researched, unbiased opinions regarding a question or an issue.

Original

People born under this sign are well known for their originality and uniqueness. They are surely one of the most unique people you will ever see, and they like to wear this fact on their sleeves.

They are innovative geniuses who love to think outside the box, especially with creative projects and finding solutions to problems. Often, Aquarians throw away the box and come up with something that can be revolutionary and path-breaking. Their penchant for revolution and novelty is also observed in their wish for a better world.

Originality and uniqueness mark the existence of all Aquarians. These factors also extend to their creative minds, so they often have various artistic tendencies. Aquarians love to use art as a medium of expression and take up media such as writing, painting, and composing.

In personal lives, Aquarians are often known as slightly (or in many cases very) eccentric, but almost all Aquarians enjoy this label. They would rather embrace their eccentricity and weirdness than lead a boring and inconsequential life.

Negative Aquarius Traits

Now that we have gone through the positive traits of Aquarius, it is time to have a look at the negative characteristics of the sign.

Cold

Aquarians may seem insensitive and cold. This is because they are less emotional and more pragmatic, which allows them a unique perspective on the world. They tend to over-analyze things, and that creates a sense of detachment from the regular world. This detached nature may make others around them feel uncomfortable. When this detachment is paired with their rigid ideas and thought processes, people often get put off.

They often run into problems due to their aloof and impersonal nature, especially when they are supposed to deal with a situation that calls for heavy emotions and sensitivity. When the situation is serious, you do not want to alienate people.

Condescending

Aquarians have a proclivity for deep thinking and ideas, which makes them one of the most intelligent signs, but this inclination also makes them susceptible to condescension. Aquarians are set in their ideas and often believe that they are correct, which automatically makes everyone else incorrect. They often fail to notice that they are talking down to a person, because they believe that their opinion is more than an opinion, i.e., it is a fact. Once an Aquarian makes up their mind, it can be downright impossible to have them change it again.

This trait can be the harbinger of the frustration of people around Aquarius, especially if they are trying to exchange ideas or propose solutions. The behavior of Aquarians can make others feel inferior.

Overly Idealistic

Aquarians are blessed with a vision that is an asset, but this asset can also turn into a curse if not handled properly. Aquarians tend to become too idealistic, which makes them chase things that are nothing less than perfect. Perfection is an impossible concept, but Aquarians may fail to realize this, which often leads to frustration, dissatisfaction, and in some cases, depression when they fail to reach the impossible and lofty standards.

Usually, their idealism can make the Aquarians slightly delusional and somewhat self-righteous.

Unpredictable

Aquarians love change and uniqueness. They often try to change for the better, but this quality can make them unpredictable. Aquarians often seem distant and emotionless; this is because they release their emotions, especially anger, in sudden, quick, and unpredictable bursts that seem to come out of nowhere.

Bad temper and anger management can be significant problems for Aquarians, especially the individuals who have to face a lot of pressure and stress. These individuals hate being emotionally vulnerable, so if something really grinds their nuts, they can lash out severely. This outburst may compensate for and include a lot of pent-up emotions.

Aquarius Characteristics in Common Situations

Sometimes Aquarians may appear to be insensitive as they face difficulty while dealing with their emotions and feelings. Their difficulty does not mean that they are not sympathetic or compassionate towards others. Aquarians can form close bonds with people (once they get comfortable with them). Here are some examples that show how Aquarians react in particular situations.

Aquarius in Love

They are all about mental and intellectual stimulation, and not surprisingly, an Aquarian person seeks the same qualities in a relationship, too. They need partners who can engage in interesting, complex, and intriguing conversations and who can tolerate their habit of going off on tangents all the time. As an Aquarian person, you can never feel romantically inclined towards a person unless they can provide you with some form of intellectual stimulation. This stimulation need not be about existentialism or the banality of evil; it can be about simple things such as video games.

Along with intellectual stimulation, Aquarians desire mental connection. They do not feel comfortable with a person unless they can form and enjoy a mental connection with them. Besides these two factors, an Aquarian also appreciates independence and honesty. An Aquarius person is incomplete without independence. They are hungry for freedom, even if it comes at the cost of being a loner. They need a sense of independence from their partner and will give the same to them. They always respect the boundaries of their partners and treat them as equals. If an Aquarius falls in love with someone, they will look at the relationship as a lifetime commitment. They won't be afraid of sacrificing to save and cherish their relationship.

If someone betrays or cheats on them, they experience anger like no other. They will most likely end the relationship immediately and move on. Aquarians don't forgive, and neither do they forget. We will discuss this in detail in an upcoming chapter.

Aquarius in Family and Friendship

Aquarians love their friends, family, and close ones. They cherish family life and enjoy people who are creative, honest, and intelligent. They are ready to make sacrifices and take risks for the sake of their family and dear ones.

As for friendship, Aquarians tend to be popular. They generally have a lot of acquaintances and are friends with many people. This is because they look at the world from a collaborative viewpoint. They possess a self-righteous and slightly condescending attitude which may make people uncomfortable, but generally, Aquarians are quirky, fun, and easy to hang around with.

Aquarians are bad with their emotions and despise being emotionally vulnerable. This may be a factor in their ineptitude at making close friends and forming personal bonds with people. They will always take time before they form a close relationship with someone. They will need ample time to process things and feel connected with someone on an intellectual and emotional level. Once you befriend an Aquarius, you will always be their most reliable friend. When someone breaks their trust, an Aquarius person goes haywire.

Aquarius Celebrities Who Espouse the Traits of the Sign

Aquarius people are known for being strong, original, and deep thinkers. They are humanitarians and are bold and dedicated.

There are a lot of advantages to being born in the Aquarius sign as it allows you to fight for causes that can change the world. They are uncompromising and can make difficult decisions. The only problem they have is they fail to express their emotions properly. Still, they can be highly empathetic towards the pains and pangs of others.

The element of air rules a lot of celebrities. Here is a list of some famous Aquarius celebrities that display many of the traits associated with the sign.

Ellen DeGeneres

Ellen has become an international star and is well known for her bold yet funny personality. She was born on January 28. She is a talk-show host, a comedienne, an actress, and a producer and is most known for her syndicated daytime talk show, The Ellen DeGeneres Show.

Along with her many Hollywood accolades, Ellen proudly displays the two remarkable Aquarius traits of philanthropy and humanitarianism. She is a staunch supporter of animal and LGBTQ rights and has started many charities. She regularly donates to various other causes, too. For her charity and related work, she has been awarded the Presidential Medal of Freedom.

Millie Bobby Brown

A young actress of considerable talent, well known for her path-breaking series, *Stranger Things*, Millie Bobby Brown is a true Aquarian. She strongly supports social justice and equality and uses her fame to make the world a better place.

She was born on February 19th and is the youngest-ever Goodwill Ambassador appointed by UNICEF. She has used her celebrity status to bring attention to the issues that plague the current generation of children and youth. Her humanitarian activities and disposition truly represent her Aquarian heart.

John McEnroe

Notorious for being the "bad boy of tennis," John McEnroe has all the Aquarius's classic traits. He was born on February 16, and is well known for his temper, on and off the court. He has had confrontations with his opponents, officials, and umpires. His "tantrums" or outbursts have made him famous with the press and social media, and these tantrums have been parodied multiple times, making him a pop culture sensation. He is an outspoken, independent, and strong-minded individual just like all other Aquarius people. He is ready to fight for the things that he believes in- literally and figuratively.

Elizabeth Banks

A progressive and talented actress, producer, and director born on February 10th, Elizabeth Banks has all the traits of an Aquarius person. She is a strong supporter and advocate of women's choice, rights, and autonomy over their own bodies. She has used her fame and power to influence people and ensure equal pay for the cast and crew irrespective of gender. She often inserts feminist and radical themes in her art pieces.

Her recent project was a reboot of *Charlie's Angels* featuring four strong female leads who bring down a corrupt organization. She drove people's attention towards women's empowerment in the film industry that has always been dominated by men.

Oprah Winfrey

One of the most recognized faces in the world, Oprah Winfrey (or just Oprah) is an embodiment of the Aquarius sign. She is an excellent listener and empathetic person. Her intuition and empathy have helped hundreds of celebrities and common individuals open up to her on her shows, such as The Oprah Winfrey Show and Super Soul Sunday. Her desire for equality allows her to look at her guests without an iota of prejudice and provide ample empathy and sympathy to them. She is empathetic towards their pain and plights. She was born on the January 29. Her other remarkable Aquarian trait is her penchant for charity.

Chapter Two: Aquarius Strengths and Weaknesses

Every person is blessed and cursed with a set of strengths and weaknesses. Individuals born under a particular zodiac sign tend to have certain similar common traits that they share. Some say that one man's food is another man's garbage. Similarly, something that is absolutely crucial for a zodiac sign can become outright trivial and despicable for another. It is necessary to understand your weaknesses and strengths that can help you lead your life in a better way. Aquarius is a contradictory sign; so, it is even more important to understand its strengths and weaknesses so that you can help yourself (or your Aquarian friend) to have a tantrum-free life.

Positive Traits

Here is a quick look at the positive traits of an Aquarius individual.

Unconventional

Aquarians are often fascinated by freedom, unconventional ideas, concepts, and technology. They are rebellious and are always in need of freedom. Their love for freedom does not mean that they do not appreciate people; rather, they like people and can appreciate innovative ideas. They love innovation and will appreciate an innovative idea, even if it is not plausible in real life.

Trendsetters

Aquarians are the trendsetters of the zodiac who love to interact with other people. The eleventh sign of the zodiac is known for its love for freedom. They may appear shy, but they can be quite lively and unconventional if the situation demands. They always focus on philosophical concepts, ideas, and feelings. This is possible due to their superior intellect, which they generally use to help others. They are not judgmental and tend to look at every side of the story before reaching a conclusion. They are adaptable, which makes them sociable, but they still prefer their solitude. They may need to go back and recharge their energy levels in solitude.

Stimulated Personality

The world is full of opportunities for all air signs, especially the Aquarius. Air signs use their minds thoroughly whenever they deal with new situations and people. Aquarians need mental stimulation; if they do not feel mentally stimulated, they get bored and lose all motivation.

Visionaries

Two planets, Saturn and Uranus, govern Aquarius. Uranus is well known for its visionary ideas and properties. These visionary ideas also make the people born under this planet visionary. This is why Aquarians are often highly intuitive and are blessed with the gift of precognition. This also makes them experts at planning things. They are versatile, powerful, bold, bright, and lovely. They are big thinkers, genuine humanitarians, and innovative workers.

Group Lovers

These people love to be alone, but they like to work in groups, which is why they often have a lot of colleagues around them.

Independence

They always strive for equality and independence. They do not like it when they are forced to stay under chains and hate it when their rights get stolen away from them. This often makes them seem detached and cold, but these two factors are just defense mechanisms against intimacy and brashness.

Charisma

They find it difficult to trust people initially, but once they learn how to do it, they can express themselves freely in a better and more guided way. This makes them highly charismatic, friendly, and sociable.

Popularity

People who belong to this sign are often popular, and they often try to make the world a better place. They do have their problems though; for instance, they may often indulge in concepts, ideas, and plans that can be unrealistic.

Communication Issues

If you are an Aquarian and find it difficult to talk to people sometimes, it is not your fault; it is your sign's personality trait. Aquarians often find it difficult to invest in emotions that make them run into communication problems. Learning how to establish connections with people and invest in emotions can help them learn more about others and improve communication dramatically.

Solitude

Their love for solitude can be taken as a negative as well as a positive concept. On the one hand, their solitude makes them seem distant and aloof, while on the other, it makes them focused, dedicated, and energized. Aquarians love to be alone sometimes, and if left to their own devices, they can bring forth new and exciting ideas.

If Aquarians are not given their space and solitude, they become cranky, and their clarity and precision of mind vanish. This often confuses their close ones as they fail to understand the reason behind this peculiar and unanticipated behavior. As an Aquarian, you must have noticed that you do not worry about giving explanations or reasons when you want to be left alone. This can startle your loved ones, and they may find it inexplicable. Avoid it.

Leadership

Aquarians are gifted with impeccable brains. They are remarkably charming, independent, and original. They pine for intellectual stimulation all the time and stay faithful to people who can provide it. These qualities make them a great team leader, despite being rebellious. Their non-conventionality makes them an inimitable leader as they come up with solutions that no one else can.

Attractive

Their charm, elucidation, boldness, and high intellect make them popular among prospective romantic partners, but surprisingly, Aquarians are more inclined towards friendship than romance. A problem that partners often face is that it is difficult to understand them. This can lead to frustration, especially if the partners do not get along with their enthusiasm and energy. Aquarians are careless when it comes to rules and norms, and that might seem distasteful to their partners.

Inventive and Active

They think continuously, which makes them active and inventive. They are always thinking of new ideas and finding new solutions to make the world a better place. They try to discover new ways to help others.

Love Changes

They not only desire change; they love it. They love to shake things just so that they can inspire others. They want to make everyone's life better, including their own.

Entertaining

They are strange, no doubts there, but this eccentric attitude makes them highly sought-after friends. They are never boring, and they generally possess a great sense of humor. They are good storytellers, and they will never bore you. They love to share their joy with others, which makes them popular with everyone.

Out-of-Box Thinkers

Their eccentricities also make them thinkers with rare precision and capabilities. They dare to imagine ideas that others simply cannot think of. They are often interested in philosophical discussions and possess an "outside the box" thinking. They often astonish others by providing simple yet effective solutions to complex problems.

Creative

They never sit idle; they always do one thing or another because they hate being bored. They are creative and individualistic.

Nice

They can seem aloof, but they are some of the nicest and caring people around.

Free Thinkers

They are great listeners and will often listen to others' opinions, but they rarely change their views about anything. They tend to stick to their beliefs and ideas, but this does not mean that they are unyielding.

Aquarius Negative Traits

It is clear from the previous section that Aquarians are blessed with a lot of positive traits that can help them change the world for good. These traits allow them to enjoy their lives thoroughly and with full dedication.

Not everything is great about Aquarians, though, as the sign also has negative characteristics. These negative traits are, in a way, a weakness for Aquarians, which often lead to problems. Getting rid of these weaknesses can make life easier for Aquarians. Here is a list of common weaknesses for the Aquarians.

Detached

They can be quite detached from the world and the people around them, which can often come off as disrespectful. As an Aquarian, it is necessary to learn how not to appear disrespectful as this trait may leave you being treated as an outcast.

Lack of Balance

This does not concern physical balance. Aquarians love taking care of their friends and family, along with other people. They are blessed with humanitarian instincts and tend to improve the atmosphere of their groups and teams. This can prove to be an asset for a team leader, but many Aquarians often forget that a team consists of separate individuals. While taking care of the team as a group is essential, it is also necessary to take care of the individuals as separate people. Each person has separate importance in your life and treating them as such will help you improve communication and relation with them. Finding the balance between the team and the individual is important.

Stubborn

They can be quite stubborn. They are dead-set on their views and opinions and do not change them no matter who tries to convince them and in what way. They will listen to the opinions of others but will strictly follow their own ideas.

Impatience

This is closely related to the previous point. Aquarians not only avoid changing their opinions or ideas, but they also tend to get impatient with people who try to change them. They hate it when people cannot understand their opinion or see their side of something.

Unpredictability

This is a pro as well as a con for the Aquarians. Unpredictability, combined with amity towards independence, may make Aquarians seem too impersonal and distant. Aquarians love their own thoughts and ideas that make them unpredictable and confusing for people who don't know them well.

The previous section covered the general traits of Aquarius. The next section will focus on specific key traits that are observed in Aquarian individuals of both male and female genders.

The Aquarius Woman: Key Traits

No sign is like Aquarius, not even other air signs. Aquarians are quite serious and connected to reality, yet they love indulging in philosophy and fantasy. Female Aquarians are powerful, almost like a force of nature, which can prove quite scary for people around her. Here are traits that can help you understand an Aquarian woman better.

Dominant Side

When you meet an Aquarian woman, let her dominant side come to the surface. This will help you understand her better. These women are generally wise, self-sufficient, and highly authentic. They tend to always be on the lookout for new ideas and freedom.

Humanitarianism

Like all other Aquarians, female Aquarians love helping others. They tend to interpret life in general in a surprisingly offbeat and out-of-the-box manner. They will amaze you with their interpretation of life. Some of the most famous Aquarian women include Rosa Parks, Virginia Woolf, Oprah Winfrey, Yoko Ono, Shakira, and Jennifer Aniston.

Independence and Mystery

A woman born under Aquarius is full of mystery, unconventionality, and passion. She loves independence. Aquarius is a fixed sign, so she doesn't like being controlled.

Helpful

They love helping others. Whenever you need advice or help, she will always be there for you. She loves caring for people and animals. She will always get involved in a cause if that can help to make the Earth and society a better place to live. She never backs down on a challenge or helping others.

Social Butterfly

An Aquarian woman loves socializing and will generally have friends from various cultures and places if her surroundings permit. She not only likes to make friends with various people, but she also tends to keep the friendships intact. She keeps her promises and is highly loyal. She is also loyal to ideas, concepts, and conditions. For instance, if she loves a restaurant or a place to eat, she will visit it frequently. In fact, she might even visit the same restaurant all the time. She is devoted and dedicated.

An Independent Lover

An Aquarian woman will be an independent lover. She loves the concept of love and may transform herself into various roles just to satisfy her significant other. She may play the sister, the mother, the provider, and even the father if the need arises.

While Aquarian women love the concept of love, they find it quite difficult to fall in love. They do not like getting attached to someone, even in love. The first few dates are used to establish trust only. Once trust is established, she may find interest in the person.

Love Hurts

Loving an Aquarius woman can be a difficult job. She is highly intelligent and independent. The partner needs to be mentally and psychologically prepared to deal with a force like her. An Aquarian woman puts a high price on communication. She is in touch with her feelings and emotions and filters them frequently to safeguard them. She is friendly, but she will never let anyone get to her with ease. As soon as an Aquarian woman falls in love with someone, she becomes the most dedicated person imaginable. It is difficult to predict her actions, which is why the other person may often feel shocked, surprised, and astonished in the relationship. For an Aquarian woman, lovemaking is cerebral, and she does not like any inhibitions; she likes to experiment a lot and will do a variety of new things in the bed.

Even in a relationship, an Aquarian woman will want and cherish her independence. She cannot tolerate a partner that does not respect her independence and self-reliance. Her ideal partner needs to be understanding, smart, and bold. They should understand the side of her that is rarely visible to anyone else.

Domesticity

An Aquarian woman is not very domestic. She needs her space and discretion in a partnership; otherwise, the relationship will die immediately. Aquarians hate tradition and an Aquarian woman will not be of the traditional type either. She will never do your laundry or cook your dinner. She is a rebel and will make her own path. The ideal partners for Aquarian women are Gemini, Libra, Sagittarius, and Aries.

Motherhood

While not all women love being a mother or want to be one, those who do can continue with this section. Aquarian mothers are full of love, but they need their own freedom. Their children often learn the importance of individuality early in their lives and know how to treat other people with respect and honor.

An Aquarian mother treats her children as equals and enjoys playing with them. She is always proud of her family and will talk about them with others quite often.

Friendly

An Aquarian woman is quite friendly and has many friends from various walks of life.

Reserved

An Aquarian woman enjoys her freedom thoroughly, which is why she may find it a bit difficult in the beginning to show her true feelings to other people. She prefers people who have the same views about freedom as her. Her group of friends generally consists of deep thinkers and intellectuals. She likes an intellectual challenge if she is comfortable with the person, otherwise, she may act reserved.

Diverse Person

They treat everyone equally, and it is no wonder that the group or social circle of an Aquarian woman will consist of people from many different walks of life. She will have all types of friends from a variety of social environments. All of them will generally have quite colorful and bold personalities. An Aquarian woman will always want a group of friends that is diverse and interesting, like her personality. For her, being multilateral is crucial. She values friendship and cherishes and celebrates her friends. She is reliable, devoted, and dedicated to her friends.

Money

They like having money, but it is just a means for achieving things, and not the goal. An Aquarian woman is not too focused on earning money; instead, she focuses more on whether she enjoys the work.

Independence and dedication allow Aquarian women to make a lot of money. She doesn't mind taking risks and is often open to a variety of new ideas. She is not mad after money, but she sure does know how to make it.

She is generous and will often donate generously to charity.

It is recommended for Aquarian women to hire accountants. Aquarians do not value money a lot and don't think of it too much. This may ruin their finances if not handled carefully.

Work

Aquarius is represented with a water bearer, i.e., the carrier of ideas; this makes the sign bold, intelligent, and creative. An Aquarian woman, too, is highly sought-after because she is imaginative and creative at her work. She knows how to make things happen and is good at being assertive and staying in control. This makes her a great boss and a brilliant leader of her people.

Colleagues and workers alike find her nice, inspiring, and dedicated. Her hard-working nature makes her a good psychologist, teacher, politician, musician, manager, social worker, etc.

Health

They are generally blessed with good health and do not indulge in exercise a lot. It is still recommended for them to follow an exercise routine to maintain their health. Aquarian women have their Achilles' heel in their heel. They should pay close attention to their ankles. She should pay attention to where she steps and should take care of her legs.

Trendsetter

They like to find and forge their own path, so you will rarely see an Aquarian woman in a regular mall buying simple clothes. She likes to buy unique pieces that look stunning and different. She doesn't like to follow trends; she would rather set her own trends. She works the clothes that she has, which is why her style is often described as interesting, courageous, and outside the box.

An Aquarian woman should wear emerald green, turquoise, and similar bright shades, as these colors are good for her. She tends to wear elegant clothes with minimal, discrete jewelry.

The Aquarius Man: Key Traits

The previous section covered details and key traits regarding Aquarian women; here is a small section covering Aquarian men's key traits.

Orders

Aquarian men hate to follow orders; don't expect them to do something just because you asked them to do it. Aquarian men are libertines, self-sufficient and highly independent. They are always looking for freedom in every situation.

Charming

Many people feel a bit overwhelmed after meeting an Aquarian for the first time. But if you give them enough time, you will be surprised by their intellect. It will charm you instantly, and you will be fascinated with his visionary, brilliant, and inventive solutions.

Unorthodox

An Aquarian man may seem slightly unorthodox initially or even later in the relationship, but this is normal. The unorthodox nature of an Aquarius man results from his unique perspective on the world. With time people learn to appreciate this uniqueness and take after him. He likes unusual things that many people are not aware of. He does not like to follow people, as he is a natural-born leader.

Innovation

An Aquarian man is blessed with extreme creativity and intellect. His ideas are often driven towards society's benefit and can bring in a change in the world if provided the proper opportunity. This superior intellect does not make him too cerebral, though, and he is more often quite down-to-earth. He will continue to be innovative and think deeply until you take away his liberty. Once you disrespect his freedom, values, and ideals, he may start to spiral downward.

Non-Conformity

An Aquarian man knows how the world works and can show you how it works if you permit him to. He will never take you to the usual places and will always try to find interesting places that sell unique things. The place will rarely have the regular and usual clientele. Aquarian men like to be non-conformists, and they will often have a curious lifestyle with a different and unusual career.

Famous Aquarius men include Thomas Edison, Bob Marley, James Dean, and Michael Jordan.

They Like Their Respect

To keep an Aquarian happy, it is necessary to respect his freedom but never overindulge it. An Aquarius man treats everything cheerfully, including love. He will generally be playful throughout the relationship and will be charming whenever necessary.

Aquarian men do not like displaying love in the usual old-fashioned ways. They may not even do the whole "I love you" routine when the time arises. This will be too conventional and normal for them. Aquarian men won't choose the usual gifts and regular dates, like flowers, chocolates, movies, etc. Expect going to old Chinese artists to get tattoos, having stars named after you, or going hiking and looking at caves.

Loyalty

An Aquarian man may be quite popular and have a lot of friends, but he is an incurable romantic under the guise of a rational person. He is an idealist, a loyal partner, and a true friend.

The large number of friends an Aquarius man has shows how popular and delightful he is. He is a diehard romantic, a rational person, a great friend, a trusted partner. He can be quite capricious, but ultimately, he is logical. His decisions may seem unusual, but they will be generally correct.

Freedom in Relationship

He prefers a relationship in which both partners respect and cherish freedom and independence. He prefers a relationship in which a partner is self-sufficient, much like him. This is often misinterpreted as a desire to have an open relationship, but this is false.

Hopeless Romantic

Aquarian men are truly passionate about their partners and will sacrifice everything, including themselves, for their loved ones. For him, great love stories such as Romeo and Juliet are fascinating. Not all Aquarian men act highly grandiose, but you will still receive unusual (often pleasant) surprises from them.

Mental Attraction and Intimacy

An Aquarian man is more interested in a person's mental and intellectual capabilities than their physical attributes. He should be able to communicate with the person and share mental intimacy. Without this, he cannot enjoy the relationship.

An Aquarius man is a true romantic who will love to show his affection from time to time.

In the Bedroom

An Aquarian man craves mental intimacy. He loves mental attraction and needs to form an intimate mental bond with the partner before anything else. He is not a laborious lover, but he will be innovative in the bedroom. He is governed by the element of Air. If you want to get to his erotic side, you will have to tap into his mental side. He loves to play mind games before anything else happens in the bedroom.

Challenges

The Aquarian man is bold and loves to try new things in and out of the bedroom. He may ask you to go with him on a marathon or jump from a plane. In the bedroom, too, he loves to try new things.

Commitment

They can be quiet, but they will always bring forth a new surprise once they trust you. It can be quite difficult to touch the core of a quiet Aquarian, but it is definitely worth the hard work. You will never regret being friends with an Aquarian.

They cherish their independence, and they will enjoy it forever. They will not commit to a person until they realize that the person is the one for them. Once he realizes that it is indeed the right person, he will commit immediately with total happiness. His partner should be understanding and intelligent.

Ideal Partner

An Aquarian wants a partner who sees life from his point of view. If he ever thinks that his independence is being threatened, he will disappear. He does not like it when things go badly, and he will show his unhappiness.

The best and most compatible signs for Aquarius are Gemini, Libra, Aries, and Sagittarius.

Visionary

An Aquarius man is intuitive and will always have solutions for problems, even if they seem unsolvable to others. An Aquarian man can be a great leader if he becomes more flexible. He is intelligent, logical, and smart, which makes careers such as a psychiatrist, engineer, financial consultant, investigator, or chemist perfect for him. He is a humanitarian at heart and desires to change the world, which means that he can be a good politician too.

Friendly

An Aquarian man has many friends and will always be interested in socializing with people. He is a social animal and quite popular with all kinds of people. While his friendliness makes him popular with a lot of people, not many of them understand him properly. He generally tends to hide his emotions and feelings and can react in a variety of ways in similar situations. He often tries to find the true feelings of his friends about him. It is recommended to indulge in this fantasy of his and see what he discovers.

Logic

An Aquarian man is driven by logic, and only logic controls his wallet. It is almost impossible to outsmart him, especially in business. He knows where and how to invest to earn the most profit. He always analyzes the risks involved in something and will invest once he understands the risks completely. He will always read the contracts before signing them.

Health

They are blessed with good health, as they are generally quite active. Excessive activity may bring problems related to the legs. An Aquarius man needs to take care of his legs.

Team Player

An Aquarius man is a team player and loves being in a team. He loves being a part of team sports and activities, as he likes to make new friends. The Aquarius man may have a lot of acquaintances, but he has only a few friends. He is a nice chap who is generally sure of himself. People may find it a bit confusing sometimes, as he tends to distance himself from others to maintain a proper relationship. He is a loyal person and appreciates and cherishes friendship.

Style

As far as style and fashion are concerned, the Aquarian man prefers clothes that portray his unique style and personality. He likes clothes that he feels look good on him and does not care about what others think. He often catches the eyes of other people with his interesting combination of clothes. If he ever wears jewelry, it is normally classy and rarely opulent.

Chapter Three: Cusps

Have you ever felt that you display the traits of two different zodiac signs? For instance, you may be born under Leo but you often show cancer traits or vice versa? You are not alone; this is a common condition known as being born on a cusp. People born on the cusp have two individual zodiac signs that work in various combinations. So, you may be born on the Leo-Cancer cusp, which means you will display related traits of both these signs.

When you are born under a particular zodiac sign, the sun is present in that constellation. The sun moves gradually between signs. If a person is born when this movement is taking place, it is said that they are born on the cusp. This allows both the neighboring zodiac signs to have an influence on the person.

The Sun's cusp period begins at 29 degrees and 30 minutes in the first sign and then goes through the next sign at 0 degrees and 30 minutes. You need to know the birth time of a person to calculate their natal chart accurately and to see whether they were born on the cusp. Due to the slight shift of astral bodies, the date varies from year to year. You can find out your natal Sun using any online sun sign calculator.

In astrology, a cusp is an imaginary line that divides two consecutive signs. The solar disc is around ½ a degree in diameter. This is convenient, as it allows the Sun to mount the cusp. The movement of the Sun allows it to be partially present on two sides simultaneously.

In simple terms, if a person is born three days before or three days after the change begins, they are born on the cusp and will display the traits of both the signs.

Cusp and Its Effects

Being born on a cusp can be quite a unique experience as it enables the person to have personality traits from both the signs, but often the energy of both the signs can compete with each other. This provides individuals with various qualities and problems. Aquarius, like all other zodiac signs, has two cusps. They are:

- Aquarius and Capricorn
- Aquarius and Pisces

Let us have a look at these two combinations.

Aquarius-Capricorn Cusp

Dates: January 16–22

The people born on a Capricorn-and-Aquarius cusp may show a lot of different sides of themselves to the public, but what matters the most is their personal and private life. Their waking dreams, inner fantasies, ideas, emotions, and feelings matter a lot to them. They are creative souls, and the workings of the inner mind matter most to them.

As their interior lives are so fascinating and rich, Capricorn-Aquarians may feel sad about or disappointed in their outside lives. They may find them constricting, dreary, dull, and lacking. They may feel a vague sense of ennui. This can lead to difficulties in their relationships. It is difficult to be with a person who loves to live in fantasy because real life can never live up to their desires.

A positive aspect of being highly imaginative is that it makes people born on this cusp quite creative. This creativity flows through them like a river.

People born on this cusp are great communicators. They love relationships based on lively intellectual discussions. This pairing of Uranus and Saturn can make for a person who is creative and emotional, but it can also lead to a desire for logic, context, and reasoning. Individuals born on this cusp are competitive and are driven by this paradox. This zeal for competitiveness combined with creativity can lead to great success if they can get past their fantasy life.

Most Capricorn-Aquarians have a lot of contradictions existing within them. They need a strong sense of security, but this desire is combined with a passion for freedom. They love learning but can feel overwhelmed by challenges. They want to change the world for the better but are often delusional regarding reality.

People born under this cusp can be quite critical, which may prove difficult for others. If you are a Capricorn-Aquarian whose critiques are usually poorly-received, try softening the blows.

Aquarius-Pisces Cusp

Dates: February 15-21

People born on this cusp are often thought to be the natural psychics of the zodiac.

They are tolerant, understanding, compassionate, and generally have extroverted personalities. They are quite sensitive. They like being around people as it can relieve stress, rejuvenate them, and offer a sense of purpose. They are often scared of being misunderstood.

People born on this cusp are goal-oriented, but they are also the biggest procrastinators. Procrastination can be built-in, which often disrupts the flow of things present in their minds. This can create a mess in their mind, but they rarely are worried about it. Their mind is as full of brilliant ideas as they are full of creative energy. This cusp is in touch with its emotional and compassionate side, which often inclines them to avoid their daily duties and chores, leading to problems later.

Neptune and Uranus rule people born on this cusp, so almost everyone loves them. They are brilliant, amazing, highly intelligent, and creative, though sometimes they feel that no one gets them. These individuals should always remember that it is not necessary for everyone to get you. The only thing that matters is that you understand them. Understanding someone can be the greatest strength a human can have.

The people born on this cusp have a brilliant mind that should be appreciated.

Capricorn-Aquarius Cusp Character Traits

The gender of the Capricorn-Aquarius cusp does not matter; they are all individuals who have been born to reform and change the world for good. They want to bring about ideal changes in the world that should have been made a long time ago. This combination of signs is quite vivid and strange, as, on the one hand, these people like to hold on to customs and traditions while on the other hand, they want to transform the world around them. The people born on this cusp tend to use their upbringing in a positive way and try to bring in changes using age-old traditions.

This cusp can be quite unpredictable because they are extremely smart and talented; in fact, their smartness can often border on insanity. They could still combine the cons with the pros and make them into "recharged pros" which can ultimately serve them better. Here is a list of positive and negative traits of this cusp.

The Positive Traits

- **Determined**: These individuals are highly determined and dedicated to goals, situations, and people.

- **Reformist**: They hate the status quo, and desire to bring changes to the world.

- **Practical**: They know how the world works, so they tend to avoid the idealistic outlook that is common with intelligent people.

- **Creative**: The elements of earth and air govern the people born on this cusp. This combination makes them quite creative and talented.

- **Visionary**: They possess an extraordinary vision and want to change the world using it. They believe that the world can be changed for the better and make it more comfortable for everyone.

- **Entertainer**: They enjoy fun and like to entertain others.

- **Disciplined**: They are highly disciplined about certain aspects of their life and tend to follow certain rules adamantly.

- **Vivid Dreamer**: Thanks to their immense creativity, they tend to look at things from a different point of view.

- **Traditional**: While they cherish a desire to change the world, they also indulge in traditions.

- **Responsible**: They are responsible and avoid pointless perceived problems.

- **Innovative**: They are innovative and can find quick solutions to difficult problems.

- **Enduring**: They have immense endurance and can work hard to achieve their dreams.

- **Multi-talented:** They are multi-talented and are interested in a wide range of topics.
- **Ambitious:** They harbor high ambitions, including how to change their environment for the better.
- **Loyal:** They are highly loyal towards their friends, family, and close ones.

Ultimately, this cusp yields a visionary, reformist, humanitarian, and philanthropist who values freedom and wants to help others achieve it. This sign is born to make a difference in society and is blessed with the qualities to do so.

This person is generally talkative and highly expressive, but he can also be reserved and shy. They have a private world full of vividness, fantasy, excitement, and eccentricity inside them. They are quite visual and love imagining things. This makes them creative and fun to be around.

They derive their inspiration less from reality than from the vivid dreams they tend to have often. This fuels their creativity and individual instinct that they convert into a medium of expression and communication. It also serves as a link between dreams and reality for them.

A lot of zodiac signs may tire of certain projects and let them go, but people born on this cusp like to fulfill every task they undertake. They possess an added supply of drive and motivation, which forces them to continue until they achieve their goal.

Perseverance is the biggest motivator for people born on this cusp. It allows them to gain power and authority. Being a fixed sign, it compels them to stay on the path towards the goal, even if the ultimate goal has no profit or gains. The Capricorn side of this cusp may ask to leave the project, but the Aquarius side will force the other half to continue for the sake of imagination and vision associated with the project.

Another trait, which is a blessing in disguise, is that the person born on this cusp has the qualities, abilities, and passion for transforming their dreams into reality. This cusp is an interesting combination of various traits including experimental, dreamer, realistic, and practical. They do not like following a well-trodden path; they would rather discover their own paths. They have curious minds and love to experiment with new ideas until they come up with something exceptionally rewarding and unique.

People born on this cusp are multi-talented. They can be a great scientist or a brilliant artist. This is why this cusp is also known as the Cusp of Genius. Their open-mindedness, combined with their radical viewpoint and creativity, makes them successful in most careers and fields.

Saturn rules both the signs present in this cusp. That planet is associated with hard work, and it is no wonder that the people born on the cusp of both these signs are dedicated and work hard.

People born on this cusp have the right amount of practicality, confidence, and caution. They have the desire to change the world, but they want to do so in a balanced and realistic way.

They are brilliant friends that never let their loved ones down. Their friends will never have a dull movement when they are around.

The Negative Traits

Here is a list of negative traits this cusp has.

- **Overcritical**: They can be overly critical of people and situations; that may alienate their friends.

- **Bossy**: They are smart, creative, and talented. These traits can often bring on judgment and bossiness.

- **Aloof:** They like solitude, which is often confused with being aloof.

- **Stubborn:** They can be quite stubborn, especially when asked to change their beliefs.

- **Secretive:** Their solitude can also make them seem secretive.

- **Harsh:** They do not mince their words, and let people know how things really are.

- **Narrow-Minded:** They do not like changing their ideas. Their love for tradition can make them a bit prudish and conservative.

- **Offbeat:** Some people may consider their uniqueness unappealing.

- **Rebellious:** They like to go against typical ideas and things.

- **Cold**: They are friendly, but they can also act cold at times, which often confuses their friends.

- **Unpredictable**: You can never predict what this person will say or do.

These individuals are determined and disciplined, which can make them quite bossy and critical towards people who are not disciplined. This demanding and overly critical attitude makes things difficult for them occasionally.

These individuals do not like being criticized. They cannot understand it when a person cannot see their point of view or share their vision. Their vision is perfect for them, and if people do not share it, they feel frustrated.

This cusp can be eccentric yet open-minded, but when their personal ideologies or beliefs are questioned, they can become narrow-minded quickly.

These individuals prefer high standards in almost everything in their life. They prefer to maintain higher standards in almost every aspect of their being. This is why they tend to be judgmental about people who do not live up to their standards and expectations.

This judgmental and overly critical nature makes it difficult to enjoy any relationship, as they always compare it with other situations.

Their offbeat and stubborn nature can be seen as rebellious, which may not sit well with a lot of people around them. They are extremely dedicated to their dreams and work towards them with a passion that makes them forget everything else. They are stubborn and do not know when and how to give up. They will leave no stone unturned to achieve something, even if it hurts them immensely.

They fear being misunderstood or not being understood at all. If they see this fear becoming a reality, they tend to enter a world of their own fantasy and diminish the reality. This is why they may often wander off into their inner world, which may make them seem harsh, cold, aloof, and secretive.

They are often said to be the life and soul of the party and enjoy social interactions a lot. But they only form good connections with people with the same intelligence quotient. This is why these individuals often find it impossible to keep personal relationships.

It is necessary for people belonging to this cusp to find a point of balance between reality and their dreams. If they do not seek this balance soon, they may become detached and depressed. This may seem quite a challenge initially, but with dedication, it can be done.

People born on this cusp are immensely interesting and fun to have around. They bring a sense of freshness wherever they go. They hate the monotony and mechanical nature of daily life and try to make it exciting and happy. They are friendly and social, but they also possess a sense of mystery around them. This is why this cusp is also known as the Cusp of Imagination and Mystery.

Aquarius-Pisces Personality Traits

People born on the Aquarius-Pisces cusp tend to be highly sensitive. They are more into their universal and personal space than world problems and concerns.

They prefer spending time with themselves to understand themselves better. It can be difficult for them to manage their day-to-day life, as it is quite a challenge to focus on mundane things for them.

These people desire experiences, but they fail to remain objective for a long time or find it difficult to do so. They are sensitive and finding a balance can be quite a task for them. For the best results, they need to learn how to put themselves out in the world and not hide in a shell. They need to learn how to feel comfortable and at ease with the world.

People born on the Aquarius-Pisces cusp are imaginative, compassionate, and sympathetic about others. They are disorganized and tend to procrastinate a lot. They may set goals frequently, but these two tendencies often result in them creating their own obstacles.

They are offbeat and eccentric, and they are unique and original. They want to change the world and are well suited to do so, as they are multi-talented. The only problem standing between them and a better world is their shy nature.

Sometimes these people are blessed with immense and incredible musical capabilities.

While they are often shy, they still love to socialize. They like to help others as the act relieves their anxiety and stress.

They are romantic and flirtatious and have genuine affection towards people. Their compassion encompasses everything. They look at the world from a unique viewpoint that others often fail to see.

People born under this sign are considered natural psychics. If they do not concentrate on these abilities right from their childhood, they may hide it and shut it down forever.

They avoid opening up to people, especially when they realize that others do not share their viewpoint and vision. They hate being ridiculed and cannot tolerate it.

This cusp is also known as the Cusp of Sensitivity. It is characterized by:

- **Sensitivity:** Those born under this cusp are quite sensitive to the emotional cues of others. They can understand what others seldom fail to realize. This sensitivity comes from their ability to see beyond the facades most of us put up.

- **Uniqueness:** The perfect amalgamation of air and water leads to a unique personality. Their ability to think and experience life is unique.

- **Tolerance:** The tolerance of this cusp is unlike any other. They are open-minded and welcome change with open arms. There is nothing even remotely narrow-minded about their thinking. This tolerance is often visible in all aspects of their lives.

- **Talent:** The Aquarius-Pisces cusps are extraordinarily creative and talented. Their tendency to let their imagination run wild is perhaps a leading reason for this.

- **Emotions:** Since this cusp is known for its sensitivity, they feel all emotions quite strongly. When surrounded by loved ones or in a happy environment, the positive vibes these individuals experience is magnified.

- **Artistic Merit:** One of the favorite artistic expressions of imagination this cusp is known for is painting or drawing. Most individuals born under this cusp have a natural inclination toward arts.

- **Dreaming:** This cusp is that of dreamers and inventors. They dream big dreams and aren't scared to chase those dreams.

- **Idealism:** This cusp is idealistic. They are strong proponents of the idea of "what should be" in all aspects of life.

- **Sensuality:** The combination of Aquarius and Pisces results in a cusp that's quite sensual. They are not only in touch with their inherent sensuality, but they aren't scared to display it.

- **Pride:** This cusp takes immense pride in their work and all other attributes of their life. Their pride doesn't translate into arrogance but shines through in everything they say and do.

- **Flirtatiousness:** The playful nature of Aquarius makes them good at flirting. The mischievous sparkle in their eyes while flirting is clear to anyone who pays attention. This desire to flirt, coupled with their sensuality, makes them skilled at flirting.

- **Loyalty:** Aquarians and Pisceans are both known for their loyalty. Unsurprisingly, the cusp of these zodiacs results in fierce loyalty. Once you have earned the trust of this cusp, they will stand by your side until you do something to break their trust.

- **Compassion:** This zodiac sign is sensitive to the emotions and feelings of those around them. So, they are naturally compassionate. They often try to do their bit to alleviate suffering and misery.

- **Practicality:** They are not just dreamers; their imagination, when tempered with a little pessimism, makes them practical.

The Negative Traits

Hypersensitivity: A similarity all those born under this cusp share is sensitivity. Even the slightest criticism is taken personally and magnified. Every comment becomes a barbed personal attack. This is one reason why this cusp is known to be quarrelsome.

- **Pessimism**: Thinking about the worst outcome in every situation might be termed as realism, but it is nothing more than pessimism. These individuals always have a "glass-half-empty" perspective toward life.

- **Secretiveness**: Playing your cards close to the chest seems to be the mantra for this cusp. They are incredibly personal and don't open up easily to others. What might seem like secretiveness to the untrained eye is merely their desire to keep things private.

- **Moodiness**: The cusp of the air and the water sign is known to be quite moody. One moment they can seem cheerful, open, and breezy, and the next, it looks like they are on another planet altogether.

- **Impatience:** This cusp is impatient. They want and expect quick results in all aspects of life.

- **Aloofness:** Aquarians are known for their aloofness. When this airy sign combines with the philosophical Piscean, the aloofness quotient increases, so don't be surprised if those born under this cusp seem too aloof.

- **Stubbornness:** It's difficult to imagine someone who shares water and air elements to be stubborn. These two elements are known to be free-flowing in nature, but the individuals with these signs have strong likes and dislike. They might not have many, but they will always stand by the ones they do have.

- **Escapism:** The active imagination of Aquarius, coupled with the dreamy side of Pisces, can result in escapism. These individuals are prone to escaping into their fantasy world or imagination instead of facing life's realities.

- **Quarrelsomeness:** Remember, the stubbornness that was mentioned? Well, the stubbornness essentially translates into strong opinions and ideas. If anyone disagrees with their ideas and opinions, be prepared for an argument. The sign is incredibly passionate about its views and will defend them vehemently.

- **Cold Personality:** The combination of air and water elements makes this zodiac cusp seem cold and distant. All this is usually the culmination of their inclination to escape the world's reality and their aloofness.

Peculiar Traits

This cusp can be quite peculiar. They love luxury, which is why they may stay in the real world just enough to enjoy this. They are very kind, and that often leads to problems as they strive hard to accommodate everyone. They do not like letting people down and tend to make many appointments simultaneously and ultimately fail to keep them all.

- They do not like talking about their failures but can exaggerate their successes and achievements.

- They love freedom and liberty. Their dreaminess, combined with their love of freedom, often drives them on the path of insight and spirituality.

- They are creatively gifted and can make stunning art.

- People love them and feel attracted to them.

If the situation is right, they may indulge in religion, science, and traveling.

Strengths

- This combination allows them to have a lot of compassion and a strikingly visionary nature.

- They can convince people to look at the world from a different point of view.

- They are not above breaking rules and can work around things just fine. This makes them the most understanding of people.

People born on this cusp tend to indulge in philosophical and spiritual matters more than real-life issues and chores. They would rather deal with their fantasies instead of keeping up daily real-world commitments; this is why they forget appointments, lose things, or show up late. They often stand people up because they cannot be bothered with real life trials and tribulations. The best advice to these individuals would be to focus on the real world more often.

Chapter Four: The Aquarius Child

Your zodiac affects you throughout your life, including your childhood. If you are an Aquarian who wants to relive their childhood and teenage years and analyze why you behaved in certain ways in particular situations, this chapter is for you. This chapter is also meant for parents or guardians of Aquarian kids and has many tips that can help you deal with them efficiently.

Like adults, Aquarian kids, too, are broad-minded and curious. They are free-spirited and are bound to create trouble for their parents.

A child born under this sign is like a loaded package. They are full of imagination, stamina, spontaneity, and stubbornness. They are sensitive and will get emotionally hurt easily. Their traits are extreme and keep on frequently changing, which is why it becomes difficult to label these kids.

Some key traits that most Aquarian kids share include:

- They are brilliant at coming up with original and unique ideas.

- They can be challenging to deal with, as they are irritable and sensitive.
- They have a lot of energy and stamina.
- They have a lot of friends and are generally sociable.
- Their future is generally bright.

An Aquarian kid can have a bright future if they are allowed to use and hone their natural talents carefully. It depends on how the parents raise these kids, as this forms the foundation of a person's character. Aquarius kids hate following orders, and you will be forced to struggle with their stubbornness in such situations. You will not be able to do anything and will get nowhere with them.

Like their adult counterparts, Aquarian kids are unique and follow their own rules and decisions. They have unpredictable personalities and tend to have a lot of mood swings. This can be quite a difficult situation for their parents. The best way to deal with an Aquarius child is by allowing them their space and time. Do not try to teach or order them in a pedantic or didactic manner. This will only increase your difficulties after you explain your point. The only way these kids will learn is with patience and freedom. Aquarius is a sign of "poles" i.e., it is composed of opposing extremes. You need to be patient if you want to get through to them.

Mood swings for adult Aquarians are commonplace, but they are even more severe in kids and teenagers due to their ever-changing bodies and brains. They can be quiet and peaceful at one moment, and the next moment, they may go berserk. They are generally intelligent kids, and sometimes they can be gifted. They have above-average comprehension skills and are full of rationality.

They are visionaries and idealists and try to set up and reach fantastic goals. They are friendly and full of empathy and compassion. This is why Aquarian kids are often the most popular kid in a social group.

They are unique and desire originality, which makes them stay away from commonplace objectives and the norm. Their personalities and goals will always be unique compared to other people. This desire for uniqueness is reflected in adulthood, too, and may play an important role in their careers.

Aquarian kids are practical, but they never forget their dreams. They might choose to be practical for a while, but they will surely circle back to their dream and try to fulfill it.

Kids love to daydream, and Aquarian kids are no different. In fact, Aquarian kids daydream more than other kids. This can prove to be problematic, especially at school. Parents of Aquarian kids often have to deal with complaints regarding lack of attention, but these complaints prove futile in view of their good grades and performance.

Aquarius is blessed with the power of intuition. Aquarian kids display a knack for clairvoyance or similar powers. They often reach a problem's solution or conclusion even before the problem is put in front of them.

Their thinking process is interesting and unique, but it can prove hectic for them if they overdo it. It may even turn out to be unhealthy and problematic.

Parents of an Aquarian kid need to help them learn how to organize their minds if they want them to develop into healthy adults. Parents need to let the genius of these kids shine among their peers. They should also focus on their physical side as the kids may avoid it altogether. Many Aquarian kids may just shy away from physical activity. Avoid allowing this.

Aquarian kids are in touch with their surroundings and are attuned to the nature around them.

Aquarian kids are sensitive, emotionally, and intellectually. They get affected by external factors with ease and are sensitive to negative criticism and comments. Negative criticism from anyone can affect their inner equilibrium severely.

Parents should be careful talking around Aquarius kids, especially when trying to help them. Do not let them feel obligated in any way, especially when you offer them any advice, as they will feel patronized. Forcing Aquarian kids to do something may lead to various long-term negative effects on these kids.

These kids are socially efficient and active, but they have difficulties in their love life and relationships. They overcome these difficulties with time; just provide them ample help and enough space and freedom to do so.

They sometimes have unrealistic visions and goals for the future. If you are worried about your kid having an impossible goal, stop worrying, as he may achieve the goal one day because of his dedication and passion.

Aquarian Baby

Parents might be surprised to see their Aquarian baby's intellect. Aquarians begin to show signs of high intelligence early in their life, which can seem quite remarkable to the people around them. Unfortunately, this high intellect is often accompanied by short temper and mood swings.

They are prone to tantrums and can easily go from zero to a hundred in a matter of seconds. Such impulsive behavior can be difficult to deal with, especially for new and first-time parents, but rest assured, the impulsiveness wanes considerably with time.

They are intelligent and keen, which will make their parents feel awesome, but it will also make other adults around them flabbergasted. Aquarian kids learn quickly and will generally succeed in most subjects. They are insightful, smart, and highly adaptable, which often surprises other people. These traits make Aquarian kids special.

An Aquarius kid's best friend and supporter is their mother. A mother can generally adapt and get on with a challenging kid. She can tolerate her child's ever-changing intellect and can teach them in many unusual ways.

It is necessary to challenge and engage an Aquarian boy constantly if you want them to reach their full potential.

The Girl

An Aquarian girl will generally be extremely interested in socializing. She is the center of gravity in all social interactions. She will be surrounded by new and old friends all the time, and they will keep on coming.

She will have many different friends over the years, but not all of them will stay with her forever. They will come and go frequently. As a parent, you need to keep a close eye on this and check the people she engages with.

Aquarian girls tend to have a daily schedule that they maintain religiously, thanks to their dedicated nature. Having a daily schedule allows her to keep a sense of stability and control, which she enjoys significantly.

She is a curious person, and her curiosity is her most dominant trait. This trait continues to be with her in her maturity too. Do pay attention to this trait, as she might explore unsuitable things at an early age.

Aquarians are born to be wild and free, and an Aquarian girl is no different. She loves adventure, and she will surely get into something that will broaden her horizons in the fields she likes. If she likes something, she will try to grow in the field.

Never take away her freedom from her, as it would be the worst punishment.

The Boy

An Aquarian boy will generally be full of energy, stamina, and a spirit of immense adventure. He will generally be hyperactive, and this will help him achieve his goals and fulfill his dreams.

Hyperactivity can also lead to chaos, which may make him a hectic and "crazy" individual. It is necessary to quell the fire inside him. He needs to learn how to control it early on. You can do this by allowing him to develop a daily schedule, which will give him a semblance of order and help him learn perseverance and patience.

Aquarians are unpredictable, and Aquarian boys are no different. They are unpredictable; they also have a lot of energy, making things difficult for their parents. Their intellect develops at a rapid pace, which is directly proportional to their curiosity about everything.

They are adventurous and may embark on surprise adventures occasionally. They will most likely not tell anyone, including their parents, about it. As a parent, it is necessary to keep a close eye on your Aquarian son lest he hurts himself.

Their personality might seem unique, strange, and downright alien to the outside world. Most of the time, they act even before they think as their mind keeps on changing continuously. This also reflects their adventurous nature.

Their adventurous nature will often lead to wanton behavior. They will break curfews multiple times. As parents, such behavior may bother you a lot, but avoid getting upset. They don't do it deliberately; they just forget to keep track of time when they are enjoying themselves.

Differences Between Aquarius Girls and Boys

There are many similarities between Aquarius boys and girls, but there are some key differences that parents should remember. Aquarius boys are smart, but they are also fickle and tend to get distracted easily. You need to help him in a non-didactic way to learn how to focus on his goals. This will keep him occupied and dedicated. Often, many Aquarius boys display symptoms of ADD or ADHD.

Aquarius girls love socializing and will focus a lot on social life. Dating and relationships can be difficult for an Aquarian girl as she can either fall heads over heels for someone or be totally distant.

Children in General

Aquarian children are highly gifted as far as team play is concerned. They are heavily into competitions and are often fierce competitors in sports that require teamwork.

They are bound to grow and flourish in most activities. They enjoy adventure and thrills of life thoroughly. They are often interested in fantasy and the supernatural, especially in animated shows, books, and movies.

They will love it if you teach them basic science tricks or magic illusions. They tend to pick things up almost instantaneously and will surprise everyone around them with their dedication and talent.

Their passion is off the charts, and they tend to forget everything while doing things that they love. They often get injured or incur bruises which they fail to notice, so keep a close eye on them.

Things That You Need To Know About an Aquarian Child

If babies could talk, the Aquarian baby would have been the philosopher/deep thinker of the lot. Aquarians are deep thinkers who can spend hours just thinking, and often overthinking things. It is an expression of their creativity. Once they do pick up some words, they will babble continuously about everything they find curious. This is just one of the many traits that Aquarian kids possess. Here is a small list of various traits you can find in Aquarius children.

They Are Quick Learners

Aquarian kids are naturally inquisitive. Their curiosity develops early on, and they are ready to learn new things. They inquire about anything and everything they do not understand and try to get to the core of everything they find in front of them. They disassemble things to learn how they function. If you ever see your kids breaking or dismantling their toys, don't worry; they are just fulfilling their natural instinct. Remember that great scientists like Thomas Edison and Galileo were Aquarians too.

They Are Empathetic

Empathy flows naturally in the veins of Aquarian children. While they are adventurous and energetic, you will never have to spend hours explaining a situation to your Aquarian kid. They are blessed with good listening skills and understand other people's feelings better than everyone else. They are brave enough to display their emotions and empathy. If you are scared or sad, your Aquarian kid will understand it immediately and try to help you get over it. They will always somehow understand what others are feeling.

They Are Fearless

Aquarian babies are adventurous and fearless. They are quick learners, but they also get bored easily and quickly. They generally look for exciting and new things constantly. They are not scared of trying new things; they seek novelty. They are open to new horizons and love to explore the unknown. This is how they make their life more interesting and enjoyable.

They Have Emotional Outbursts (Short-Lived)

Aquarians are born empathetic, but this empathy also makes them quite emotional. When they come face to face with challenges, they tend to lose their balance. Once they lose this balance, they may have significant emotional outbursts. These emotional outbursts can be scary, but they are almost always short-lived. Your kid will come back to their normal self in little to no time. This shift might surprise new parents as they will not understand the ultimate reason behind the outburst, but in most cases, your kid will let you know the reason on his own after some time.

People's Person

Aquarians love communicating and socializing with others, and Aquarian babies are no different. They are great at forming connections; that is why they tend to become friends with people quickly. They are always there to help a friend or a family member. They are friendly towards strangers too. An Aquarian kid will be exceptionally outgoing right from the start. Don't be shocked if they start smiling or talking to people right from a young age.

Aquarius Babies Are Full of Surprises

Parents of Aquarius babies are often surprised by seeing the traits of their babies. They are empathetic, social, fearless, and full of adventurous spirit. They often react in an unexpected manner and generally have wacky and bizarre answers for problems and their actions. Some people call them absent-minded while others call them dynamic, but ultimately, their brain works in a way that no one else can understand.

They Are Highly Energetic

The energy of an Aquarius kid knows no bounds. They are never tired of contemplating or thinking over a problem. Similarly, they do not tire of listening to their friends constantly blabbering about random stuff. Even after doing this, they will still have enough energy to play a sport or finish their homework. They are quick, and most people lag behind while they scoot ahead.

They Are Stubborn

Aquarius kids can be quite stubborn, which can cause a lot of problems for their parents. They don't let anything or anyone affect them, as they look at the world from a positive viewpoint. They are adventurous and free-spirited, which means they would rather do things of their own accord. They do not like being controlled and like being free all the time. If you want your Aquarius kid to do something, try to inculcate a sense of responsibility in them without being too pedantic or didactic. This will help them learn what is good for them. Never order or force an Aquarius kid to do something; they will not do it, and even if they do it, they will feel alienated and will begin to despise you.

They Are Strong-Willed Too

Aquarius kids are stubborn, and their stubbornness makes them highly strong-minded and strong-willed. They will focus on a goal with full dedication until they achieve it. This is one of the most important traits of an Aquarius baby as it generally drives them. They will not hesitate to give their best and put in every effort to achieve what they want.

They Know Their Likes and Dislikes

Aquarius babies know what they like and what they do not like. They not only know about their likes, but they are also serious about them. Aquarians are generally quite individualistic, and this trait is also present in the kids. It is almost impossible to persuade them differently once they make up their mind.

Interests and Hobbies

Aquarius kids are interested in almost anything that they can get their hands on. Their hobbies are varied and highly distinct, often borderline unique. They love all games and hobbies that allow them to play with other people and interact with them. They also enjoy activities that help them channel their creativity and learn new things. They develop an interest in new things almost instantaneously because they understand that the activity has some potential for entertainment.

One thing that binds all Aquarian children is "fun"; if an activity entertains them, they will love it, and if the activity bores them, they will get rid of it. This is why they have so many different hobbies and interests. Aquarius babies and kids get bored of things easily and move on to new ones quickly.

Making Friends

For Aquarian kids, making friends is not a big deal, as they tend to have good social and communication skills. They are highly sociable, and they like all kinds of friends. They will become friends with almost anyone, anywhere.

They are rarely worried about friends that are not like them, or about friends who do not meet them often; they will still try to be friends with them. Many Aquarians have made life-long friends in schools, but this does not mean they do not enjoy short-term friends as well.

At School

Aquarius is a sign blessed with immense intellect and smartness. Aquarius kids, too, are quite intelligent but what holds them back is their desire for freedom, and sometimes laziness.

Aquarius is a hardworking sign, especially if the person likes what they are doing. Aquarian kids do a lot of hard work, but most of the time they do not like to put effort into things that bore them, including homework. They will excel and achieve the highest grades in subjects that they find interesting, but they may even fail the classes they do not like or find boring. Often this may confuse the parents and frustrate them. A lot of times, due to ignorance, Aquarian kids are labeled as being apathetic or even dumb, but this not the case. These kids understand the subject matter of the classes they fail but they just don't want to put effort into studying for the tests or do the homework on the subject.

Independence

Aquarius kids are extremely independent. As soon as they learn to walk, they start getting away from their parents and everyone else to enjoy their freedom. They always want to do something on their own or with their good friends and close social circle. They love their parents, but they would rather enjoy things on their own. They do not like being dependent on their parents.

The older they get, the less they will depend on their parents. They would rather join clubs, school organizations, etc., and get on with their friends. They learn driving early on so they can move around on their own. They love leading their own lives and do not like others interfering in it.

What to Expect When Raising an Aquarian Child

Expect the Unexpected With an Aquarius

Always expect the unexpected while raising an Aquarian child. Your child will always keep you on your toes. They are full of intelligence, emotions, and energy, and love to be on the go all the time. They like meeting new people, visiting new places, trying new things, etc. They will mostly be busy and highly active all the time. They are fearless and adventurous. Always be ready for something new and exciting while raising an Aquarian kid.

They're a Little Absent-Minded

These kids can be quite absent-minded. Many parents often complain that their Aquarian kid does not hear them. They feel that the kids do this on purpose, but this is untrue. The kids may hear their parents but simply forget it, thanks to their absent-mindedness. Their brain moves at such a pace that they forget things frequently.

You may feel ignored while dealing with an Aquarius, but most of the time, their absent-mindedness is not deliberate. It is just too difficult for the kid to keep track of their thoughts all the time.

Aquarians Are Focused

Aquarian kids are dedicated, focused, and often stubborn. They do not give up until they can maneuver according to their desire. This stubbornness may often work against them; as a parent, try to control it subtly. Sometimes, let them be stubborn, as the experience will help them learn a lesson on their own, which will stay with them forever.

Roller Coaster Emotions

Aquarius is a sign full of contradictions, and Aquarius kids are no different. One moment they may be happy, laid-back, and carefree, but the next moment they may go berserk and spiral down hard. This is normal, as a lot of things can trigger their emotions. Everyone hates being exposed to the unexpected, but Aquarians tend to take things to the next level. They have extreme reactions. Most of these emotions disappear quickly.

Aquarians Are Empathetic

If you ever feel out of your element or feel depressed and are in need of kind words or a hug, your Aquarian kid will always be there for you. They will always be the first to understand what you are going through and to try to help you. They possess the almost uncanny ability to guess how others feel without needing to be explicitly told. This is why parents of Aquarian kids are advised to control their disciplinary methods, as your kids already probably know how upset or angry you are. Use gentle words to make them understand that their choices were troublesome and that they should learn how to make them better in the future.

Aquarius Love People

Aquarian kids are highly social because they are warm, charming, friendly, and engaging. They love all forms of positive attention and like to know the people around them. You can see how social your child will be right from an early age. Babies begin to smile at random people all the time from a young age.

Quick Learners

Aquarian kids are smart and quick, which can be a blessing and a curse for the parents. The kids can figure out a lot of things early on. They are not only book-smart, but most are also socially smart. They are generally the teachers' pets (if they find the subject interesting). Your Aquarian kid needs to feel challenged all the time; otherwise, they may grow lazy and stop caring.

Idiosyncratic

No one can figure out an Aquarian, not even their own parents. They will always march to the beat of their own drums and will always do the things they believe are the best. It can be difficult to understand the motive behind whatever they do, so it is necessary to keep communication open all the time. They will always be full of surprises and sometimes shocks. Always expect an enjoyable, wild, and rewarding ride while raising an Aquarius child.

Tips and Tricks

Toys for Aquarian Kids

While Aquarian kids will love to play with almost anything that they get their hands on, there are certain toys that they will enjoy much more than other objects. These include fairy wings, musical instruments, costumes, boxes, etc.

All these toys can help your Aquarian child to think and imagine new and exciting ideas. Aquarians love to make their own games, and these items will serve as props for their games.

Activities for Aquarian Kids

Aquarian kids are full of intelligence, imagination, and passion. They enjoy a variety of activities that tap into their creativity and thinking. Such activities include creating art and reading books. Aquarius kids all love to socialize and play with their friends on the playgrounds.

Aquarius kids love socializing, but they also enjoy the peace of solitude. This is why parents should try to provide the kids with ample time to recharge themselves. This includes solo time, playing by themselves, and allowing their imagination to take over the world when the adults are out of earshot. These activities will help the Aquarius kid grow and develop. Here are some activities that will help your Aquarian child enjoy their lives and grow.

Reading

Aquarius kids are artistic, intelligent, and imaginative, so not surprisingly, they are often fascinated with stories and tales. They generally enjoy stories with children from various parts of the world, fables, and fantasies. Aquarians like to identify the differences and similarities between their experiences and the experiences of other people. They like to imagine living in different countries and worlds and think about experiences that differ from their own. Some books that they will absolutely love include:

- Alice in Wonderland by Lewis Carol
- Dreamers by Yuvi Morales
- Jumanji by Chris van Allsburg

All About the Aquarius Teenager

Aquarius teens, like Aquarian kids and adults, are unique, independent, and remarkable. They are also full of hormones and thus may drive the parents crazy in a new way every day. They don't mean to annoy parents deliberately, but they often get annoyed at people who don't tend to live up to their fullest potential. They can often misinterpret situations, sometimes without understanding the nuances thoroughly. For instance, if you come back from the office after a fairly busy day and complain about your office, they may think that you are not comfortable at the job and are selling out. They may not even look at all the positive reasons why you are doing the job, which obviously includes a paycheck.

Aquarius individuals are smart, but they tend to look at the world from a black-and-white perspective when they are teenagers. It is necessary to remind them occasionally that the world is not black and white; rather, most of it is gray. Aquarians are well known for their idealism, so don't shrug it away completely; instead, try to present the opportunities that can help them change themselves and the world around them. Allow them ample opportunities where they can volunteer to make a difference in the world. They will enjoy bringing about a change in the world.

Aquarian kids and teens have a strong sense of social justice, and they believe that the world can be changed for good. They do not like being talked down to. If you show you respect for them, they will respect you back.

Aquarius teens tend to have a lot of friends, just like their adult counterparts. They are smart and unique, but they need to have some structures and rules. Don't make the rules and lay them on them; aquarian teens will never follow rules that are forced on them. This will only lead to frustration for all those involved and may deteriorate the relationship between you. Instead, allow them to collaborate on making rules and setting up guidelines. These guidelines and rules should make sense to them, and they should feel they have put a lot of input into them. They are more likely to follow such rules without feeling angry or frustrated. Remember, Aquarians are autonomous and unique beings; the more you respect their autonomy, the more they will respect you.

Aquarius Teen's Likes

Aquarius teens are often polymaths, and they love a variety of things and fields. Some of the most highly-appreciated fields include:

Learning

An Aquarian teen will always enjoy learning new things and experiences; however, they may not feel comfortable with the school's rigidness. They like to learn on their own time and accord. They like reading books, enjoy making connections, and are passionate about figuring out new things and discovering new ideas.

Music

Every teenager loves music, but Aquarius teens love it with heartfelt passion. For them, music is life. They believe that songs and musical pieces can represent them in a much better way and can portray how they feel accurately.

Independence and Autonomy

For an Aquarius teen, their autonomy and independence are the most crucial objects. When they begin to learn that they are different from their parents and can make different life choices and enjoy different things, it provides them an almost surreal experience. Allow the teens to experiment as much as they want; encourage that behavior. Allow them to grow and let them find their own path with full passion.

An Aquarius Teen's Dislikes

Rules and Lack of Independence

An Aquarian teen abhors lack of independence. They will despise you if you use phrases such as "Because this is my house" or "Because I said so." They will never follow a rule that is forced on them. If you want them to follow the rules, allow them to collaborate on the process.

Cliques

Aquarians love to make a lot of friends, but they are ultimately lone wolves. They do not like being associated with a specific group and like to enjoy their freedom and independence. Instead of aligning with any one group, they prefer to float between different people and cliques. This makes them popular with almost everyone.

Privacy

Aquarian teens tend to be messy (all teenagers do) but never trespass on an Aquarian's privacy, or they will hate you forever. Entering the private space of an Aquarian is an invasion of their privacy. They will find it frustrating and annoying. Always seek their permission if you want to enter their private life or space. Respect their boundaries.

Chapter Five: Aquarius and Friendship

Aquarians are extroverts and are ready to make friends. They love adventure and always want to try something new with their friends. An Aquarian's social circle is filled with people who love their loyalty and charm. Most people are drawn to them since they exude a feeling of compatibility. Sometimes, people may wonder if an Aquarian is interested in them or cares for them, since Aquarians can seem disinterested and detached.

Aquarians As Friends

The Aquarius zodiac sign is the eleventh zodiac sign, and it is a sign found in the natural zone of social activity and friendship. It is easy for Aquarians to make new friends, and they are ideal friends. They are good at conversing with anybody around them, but they have only a few friends close to their hearts. Aquarians are amazing people, but they have many positive characteristics that people want to have in their companions or friends.

Aquarians are Loyal

If you have an Aquarian as a friend, you already know how lucky you are because they are the most loyal friends. An Aquarian is very supportive, and he ensures that you push yourself to meet your goals. If an Aquarian knows how passionate you are about achieving your goals, then he will do everything in his power to help you achieve them. They are never jealous of the people around them. Aquarians are good at cheering people up if they are having a bad day.

Love to Make Conversation

An Aquarian is great at conversing with people around them. If you meet an Aquarian at a party, you may talk to them for hours, and you may never know what got you started. Aquarians have the most interesting things to say to the people around them. They also ask the right questions because they want to learn more about people. Some may find Aquarians overbearing, and some Aquarians do not listen or cheer you up. There are others who may not want to help the people around them. Aquarians may want to take matters into their own hands whether or not someone asked them for help. What they fail to understand is that not everybody may want this help.

Love Fun

Since Aquarians love adventure, they are often unpredictable. You may think you know what an Aquarian wants or loves, but then they may say or do something that shocks you. They may seem a little crazy because of their spontaneity, and they love doing anything thrilling, adventurous, and interesting.

Idealists and Rebels

Aquarians are not traditionalists, and they hate following conventions. They accept no situation or explanation blindly. They always look for loopholes in the system and are not pushy people, unlike Aries and Leos. Their mantra is to live and let live. Aquarians are exceptionally kind, and this characteristic attracts people to them. They have humanitarian beliefs, and they are concerned about people's welfare. They rarely get too involved in relationships since they do not want to lose their freedom or independence.

Unconventional

Aquarians are unconventional and free spirits. Their habits and attitudes make them the most eccentric people. They are known for thinking outside the box and constantly looking for something new to do in life. They hate being bored. The combination of their kindness, love, and original thoughts makes them the best leaders. Their free spirit is as contagious as their positivity. If you hate your routine and want to spice up your life, you need to find an Aquarian friend.

Aquarius and Friendship

Aquarius and Aries

An Aquarian can communicate with an Aries easily. Aries are impulsive individuals, and this works in an Aquarian's favor since the latter loves adventure. An Aquarian and Aries can embark on long adventures together, especially those that involve dangerous activities such as bungee jumping, cliff diving, parasailing, and more. An Aquarian may tire of an Aries because the latter put themselves above everybody else. When they spend time away from each other, they understand how much they need each other.

Aquarius and Taurus

An Aquarian is in awe of a Taurean because the latter is loyal above everything else. Taureans are as true as they can be. An Aquarian and Taurean are both devoted to their friends and loved ones, and they will do their best to maintain a relationship. An Aquarian and Taurean will stick together through thick and thin. While Aquarians love crowds and noise, a Taurean is materialistic. They have a lot of fun when they spend time together, especially when they are the only two. The two may enjoy activities such as hiking and rowing.

Aquarius and Gemini

A Gemini and Aquarian bond well because Geminis are satisfying, encouraging, and stimulating friends. These qualities make it easy for an Aquarian to motivate a Gemini to try different activities. Since the two are always curious and energetic, they will try anything new. Geminis have a huge friend circle but are only close to some people, and an Aquarian is one. This is only because an Aquarian can fuel a Gemini's enthusiasm to try something new. Since an Aquarian expects people to arrive on time, a Gemini may need to work on this to maintain his friendship.

Aquarius and Cancer

An Aquarian may have difficulty in understanding his Cancer friend. An Aquarian enjoys challenges, so he may try his best to maintain his friendship with a Cancer. Since both Aquarians and Cancers have different wants and needs, it is hard for the two to maintain a relationship. Cancers love attention, but Aquarians want to be intellectually stimulated. Since Cancers have a sense of humor, they can sway an Aquarian's affections towards them. If Cancers can control their need to be loved, they can have a stable relationship with Aquarians; otherwise, the relationship will cease to exist soon.

Aquarian and Leo

It is difficult for people to not like Leos, but an Aquarian is the complete opposite of a Leo. Since Aquarians prefer to rest and relax, they rarely see eye to eye with a Leo, with a larger-than-life attitude. However, an Aquarian in the presence of a Leo is more enthusiastic than ever. Aquarians are great at keeping Leos in check. Since both signs enjoy activity, they may love brisk walks in the park or a workout at the gym. They may also have fun when they go to opera performances and rock shows. Leos and Aquarians, however, need to work together to keep their relationship going.

Aquarius and Virgo

Aquarians are attracted to Virgos since the latter are insightful and intelligent people who can intellectually stimulate an Aquarian. Virgos are very particular about some things in life and may be fussy occasionally, especially about things that do not matter to an Aquarian. Virgos are people who love ironing their clothes, combing their hair frequently, and washing their hands until they are spotless. An Aquarian may not even be able to find a pair of socks in their cupboard. If an Aquarian and Virgo can overlook these characteristics, they can have a long-lasting friendship.

Aquarius and Libra

Aquarians and Librans are naturally attracted to each other, and the relationship between them is amazing to behold. Since both enjoy crowds and social gatherings, they often meet each other at parties. They discuss new ideas, the news, and other trends and soon develop a friendship. Librans are impressed by an Aquarian's understanding of any subject. Since an Aquarian pays undivided attention to anybody he is talking to, a Libra finds it easy to talk to him. A Libra is conscious about their appearance, and this can strike an Aquarian's nerve. If an Aquarian can overlook these characteristics, the friendship between a Libra and Aquarian can last for a lifetime.

Aquarian and Scorpio

An Aquarius and Scorpio may not get along with each other. There is a lot of tension in this relationship, and it is why most Aquarians and Scorpios do not like being with each other. Aquarians never know what their Scorpio friends are thinking. They constantly wonder about their feelings and motives, which is often a refreshing change for them. Scorpios also enjoy spending time with Aquarians since they cannot figure them out. Each tries to decipher the other like a puzzle. Both Aquarians and Scorpios are stubborn, and this can lead to arguments and issues. However, it is easy for them to maintain their friendship if they will give each other a chance.

Aquarius and Sagittarius

Aquarians love hanging out with Sagittarians. They are the best people in the whole world, according to Aquarians. Sagittarians have an open mind, an adventurous heart, and a free spirit, and they love spending time with Aquarians because of their humanitarian beliefs and adventurous spirit. Since both Aquarians and Sagittarians are social animals, they may often meet each other at a party. They are probably the last people to leave the party. They love playing sports that require quick reflexes. Sometimes, an Aquarian may find a Sagittarian's honesty annoying while a Sagittarius may find an

Aquarian's failure to notice changes annoying. The two can, however, work together and have a strong friendship if they understand each other.

Aquarius and Capricorn

Aquarians love experiments, and they may develop a relationship with a Capricorn as an experiment. While Aquarians love new things and experiment with a lot of things in life, Capricorns prefer the old ways. Aquarians love change and they hate routines, unlike Capricorns. Aquarians may think that Capricorns are ruining their lives, but then the latter may do something that would help you remember why you are fond of them. Capricorns always bring some consistency to an Aquarian's life, while an Aquarian brings some life and excitement into a Capricorn's life.

Aquarius and Aquarius

Aquarians are compatible with each other, and most Aquarians feel normal when they are around other Aquarians. They are as normal as they can be around Aquarians. Since another Aquarian cannot find the love for chocolates or sardines strange, they are often happy and calm. The friendship between two Aquarians is never boring because both are adventurous. They never tire of discussing any topic and may enroll themselves to work for charitable causes.

Aquarius and Pisces

An Aquarian and Piscean can get along easily since they both have the same humanitarian instincts. If an Aquarian and Piscean get together, they will champion the group's underdog. Aquarians and Pisceans may often meet at a rally or fundraiser. They are drawn to subjects such as numerology, tarot, and astrology. Aquarians are drawn to Pisceans, who understand these subjects. They also are musical and may enjoy sharing music or plays together.

Aquarians at a Party

Aquarians are worldly, and they love speaking to people. They enjoy intellectual conversations, and they often flex their intellect. Aquarians enjoy small groups where they can show off their skills. They enjoy debates and discuss various subjects. Aquarians love to go out by themselves also. They may go for a spirit or wine tasting, a lecture, a fancy dinner, or even a concert. They only want a place where they can voice their opinions. They can discuss their opinions even with complete strangers.

Friendship Style

Since Aquarians love being around people, they are always open to meeting new people. They want to listen to their stories. An Aquarian never feels out of place even when they find themselves in a group of new people. Since they are good listeners and always ask the right questions, they can always bring people out of their shells. People may tell Aquarians things they have told nobody before. Aquarians, however, are private. They never tell people what they are thinking about or how they feel, but it may appear that they have told people everything they need to know.

Aquarians like large groups, but they take a while to find close friends. They take time to trust anybody. They take friendships seriously, and if they are disappointed, they will take it hard. They do not take it too hard if you forget to meet them for coffee, but it will take you longer to become a part of their circle. Since Aquarians always see the best qualities in people, they are often frustrated when people cannot see those characteristics in themselves.

Aquarians often feel like cheerleaders because they like to mentor people. They, however, wish there were someone in their life who would mentor them. Aquarians love to have fun, and they are always up for an adventure.

Who is the Best Friend for an Aquarian?

Since both Aquarius and Libra are air signs, they love cultural events, spending hours debating ideas, going to rock concerts, and other fun activities. Librans are more diplomatic when compared to other people, and an Aquarian knows how to call that out. They can make Libras stick to their guns and be less diplomatic. Librans know how to break an Aquarian's barriers down easily and help them trust people more. The two signs do not have a friendship based on words, and they are happy to be together even in silence. Since both Aquarians and Librans do not hold grudges, they are easy people to be with. They understand that they each need space and have enough going on in their lives. They can pick up exactly where they left off, even if they do not speak for days or weeks. Aquarians and Librans are not known for their humor, but they can laugh for hours together.

How to Become Friends with an Aquarian

Aquarians love social gatherings and are extroverts. People often surround them, and it is easy for people to get charmed by an Aquarian's characteristics. To be friends with an Aquarian for long, you need to stick around. Be there through good and bad times. Aquarians love consistency, and when you see them at the same place repeatedly, try to break the barriers down. You can have a casual friendship with Aquarians since they are nice. If you make them laugh, they will appreciate you more. If you want a deeper friendship, you need to scratch below the surface.

How to Continue Being Friends with Aquarians

Always be the best version of yourself to be friends with an Aquarian. Aquarians do not have any time for people who are not happy with their lives. They often forgive people who forget to respond or forget their birthdays, but they never like people who are mean or lie. Hurtful words and gossip, whether directed at Aquarians or others, does not impress an Aquarian.

Tips On How to be Friends with Aquarians

In this section, we will look at ten tips to help you be friends with Aquarians.

Always Be Genuine

Since Aquarians are serious, sincere, and reflective people, they will run away from you if you are insincere. They cannot respond to disingenuous flattery, and they always know who is being honest and who isn't. If you know an Aquarius, then you should compliment them on their commendable traits. This will always have a stronger effect on Aquarians since they know that you genuinely care for them. When giving gifts, you should never shower an Aquarius with flashy or expensive items.

Get to Know Them

You should never rush things when learning more about Aquarians. They always have their guards up so it takes a while for you to learn more about an Aquarian. You need to give an Aquarian the time to understand you and feel safe around you. It is only when this happens that they will slowly open up to you. Since Aquarians are playful and love adventure, they will joke around with you.

Philanthropy

Aquarians may sometimes seem detached and cold because they do not like opening up easily. They do, however, quickly attach themselves to strangers and understand their concerns. They will also do everything in their power to help them. Aquarius may have a million problems in their head, yet they will do help someone in need. They will always give them their shoulder to cry on. To befriend an Aquarian, you need to be philanthropic.

Learn to Debate

Since Aquarians are strong-willed, they will do whatever it takes to see something through if they believe in it. They will do this even if people have a different perspective. This does not mean they are argumentative or stubborn, but it is only because they are passionate about what they believe in. If you want an Aquarian to see your side of the story, use a combination of sources and facts. He may apologize to you for not seeing things the way you saw them.

Never Lie

Aquarians always want the truth, and they can spot liars instantly. If they sense you are lying to them, they will no longer want to be around you. They are this way because of their loyalty. They have strong morals, and they expect their friends to have the same morals. You will never get a second chance with an Aquarian if you are dishonest with them. If you cannot meet your friend for coffee, tell them why and have the proof needed for the same.

Quick Wit

Aquarians are charming, smart, witty, and sarcastic. If you cannot entertain them or converse with them for hours together, or talk about worldly affairs, then you cannot hold their attention. You also need to tolerate their sarcasm and know when they're just pulling your leg. If you can do this, they will want to be around you.

Learn to Love their Views

Since most Aquarians find themselves in an existential crisis, it is important for you to support their views. They are philosophers, and they often want peace and harmony in their lives. When they listen to a tragedy or remember something that happened to them, they question everything about their lives. Most people may find this childish, but to befriend an Aquarius, you need to trust them and their ideals. If you do this, they will love you, endlessly.

Trust Them

Aquarians never like feeling trapped, and if you try to control them, they will run away from you. You need to be secure to win an Aquarius over. If you question everything they do or say, they will pull away. Since Aquarians have morals and are loyal, they will do nothing to break your trust. So, learn to trust them.

Never Give Up

It does take Aquarians a long time to let their guard down. They are afraid to let people around them know how they feel or what they are going through. When this happens, you will be glad to have them for a friend. Aquarians hate rushing into relationships, but they will stick with you forever if you try hard. However, they fear commitment, but if you love them, fight for their friendship. Let them feel secure.

Prepare for a Long-Term Friendship

When you win an Aquarius over, it means they have let their guard down. This means you never have to doubt their dedication to your friendship. Aquarians are spontaneous, and they will show you their love with sentimental gifts. They always think about what they can gift you. They lift your spirits up and encourage you to follow your passions and dreams. Since Aquarians are verbal, they will remind you about your worth. Once you develop a bond with an Aquarian, it will never break. If you do not break their trust, they will never break yours. So, stick to them, and trust them. Be there to lift their spirits because they always do it for everybody. Be their mentor and friend. You will never lose them.

Chapter Six: Aquarius in Love

Let's take a look at the love compatibility of Aquarius with other signs of the zodiac:

Aquarius and Aries

The sexual relations between Aquarius and Aries can either be exciting or stressful. These two signs get along and are supportive of each other. Both signs can follow each other with a lot of energy. However, there could be a lack of emotion with intimacy or sexual relations between the two. Aries is a sign of a lot of passion and warm emotions. Their relationship with Aquarius has the possibility of bringing out the worst in their nature. It will emphasize that the cold and unemotional Mars rules Aries.

Although this might make their relations more exciting, it will fail to bring fulfillment to either of them since they both need to feel loved. There are too much energy and masculinity in this relationship, and this could cause turbulence. It is easy to understand their roles since Aquarius has crazy ideas and widens the horizons for their partner while Aries has a lot of stamina and gives off energy. At the beginning of the relationship, things could be a lot of fun for them. However, it gets tiresome with time, and there aren't enough crazy ideas to fill the empty hole of emotions.

Aries places a lot of importance on trust, and it is easy for Aquarius to understand this. Although it doesn't mean that Aquarius will remain faithful to their partner, they might instead bring up the option of an open relationship and be honest about any indiscretions to Aries. However, this is not an option for Aries, who is ruled by Mars and wants to be the center of their partner's world. This kind of relationship will only make Aries possessive and angry as they obsess over every move made by Aquarius. Other than fidelity, trust is not an issue for this pair. They both see no need for lies since the truth can be much more interesting and easier to deal with. Both signs don't feel the need to avoid conflict, and like speaking their mind. They know that any argument or conflict can be carried out constructively so that it helps them understand their partner better and makes their relationship stronger.

The conversations between Aries and Aquarius can be so interesting that most people would want to join in. Aquarius is aware of the fact that Aries is usually serious and has boundaries that need to be respected. In turn, they like making their Aries partner laugh and let loose more. For Aries, this kind of open-minded and constantly changing partner is unimaginable at times. This is why they often end up idolizing Aquarius and love entering into any dialogue with them. For Aquarius, it is a huge boost to their ego. Since both signs are strong by nature and very energetic, they could constantly end up fighting. However, they will also overcome such fights and cherish each other at the end of the day.

Aquarius and Taurus

Taurus is a sign with a slow and tender nature, which finds the unusual and changeable nature of Aquarius annoying. These two signs are rarely attracted and find each other crazy or boring. However, if they are more open-minded about unusual sexual relations, they can help each other grow a lot. The tender nature could help the distant and independent Aquarius become more motivated and creative. This, in turn, could help Taurus become a lot more productive. If these signs are respectful enough towards each other and share their emotions, they could have a great sex life. But it rarely gets this far since these signs look for very different things in their relationships. Aquarius likes being free of any attachment while Taurus looks for an unbreakable and secure bond. It can be difficult for both parties to find a meeting point.

Aquarius often stresses out Taurus, and this tends to prevent them from being honest and true to their partner. It is difficult for Aquarius to understand the fear that Taurus has of not being good enough. Aquarius doesn't indulge in self-criticism or guilt like Taurus constantly does. Taurus finds it even more difficult to express their feelings to Aquarius because the latter's strict opinions can scare Taurus away. All of this leads to an endless circle of mistrust and lies. Aquarius seems to lack flexibility even though they make it seem like they are accepting of differences in other people. For there to be trust between these signs, Taurus has to be braver and not fear the consequences of saying the wrong thing to their partner. Aquarius has to be more compassionate towards Taurus and get rid of their self-righteous attitude.

One is an Air element, while the other belongs to the earth. This is why these two signs will find it very difficult to find something in common to talk about. Taurus is the sign of Uranus' fall, which acts as a sieve for all their Aquarian partners' bright ideas. Although this may not pose a big problem, Taurus's narrow-mindedness can make their partner feel like none of their dreams will ever come true. Taurus has to be more understanding of the need to fly that Aquarius has. If they do this, they can help Aquarius work on materializing these flighty dreams. This happens rarely since Aquarius does not find it easy to talk to or open up to Taurus. It is difficult for these two signs to reconcile, and any small issue can become big for them.

Aquarius and Gemini

Verbal stimulation can make it possible for these two signs to have good sexual relations. They don't feel the need to be free of clothes to have sex but will mostly end up without them. Both signs are more focused on finding kindred spirits, and while they continue the search, they want to have a good time. The intellectual side of this relationship will be arousing for both partners. Neither Aquarius nor Gemini like being in a relationship with a partner whom they consider stupid. Being with someone without wit would be considered only an insignificant encounter for them. Aquarius is more dominating since Gemini can be shy in certain situations, and this helps Gemini become a lot freer in expressing themselves. But if there is a lack of emotion or true intimacy between them, their relationship will fall apart as they look for it in another partner.

For this couple, trust can be a strange thing. Not that they won't trust each other, because they will. Gemini rarely feels the need to lie, and Aquarius finds dishonesty ridiculous. However, Aquarius also likes privacy, but this pair will not struggle with trust issues.

Onlookers will find a debate between this pair quite interesting. Aquarius and Gemini can have extremely stimulating conversations. The humane and rational belief systems of Aquarius will be fascinating for Gemini, while Aquarius will get a chance to relieve their ego issues.

Aquarius and Cancer

Cancer and Aquarius will have a very stressful sexual relationship. Cancer is usually the most sensitive sign, but they become quite distant and rough when they want to set boundaries. Aquarius is an innovator but tends to be set in his ways and is unchangeable. Sexual relations between the two could be stressful for Cancer, and this will make them set boundaries. Aquarius, on the other hand, will find it difficult to change just to make their Cancer partner more comfortable. Cancer cannot understand the need for Aquarius to use sex in order to feel more grounded. For them, sexual relations should only have emotions involved.

Usually, Cancer is honest and loyal. However, if they fear hurting their loved ones or fear an aggressive reaction from them, they could turn to lies. The stress in this relationship could make it difficult for Cancer to share their thoughts or feelings with Aquarius, and this can lead to trust issues between the two. Although neither partner likes lying, they have trust issues since they don't have faith in their future together.

Aquarius and Leo

Opposite signs have a lot of attraction towards each other, and this is evident between Leo and Aquarius. Aquarius seems to exist to bring down Leo, who is the king of the signs. There is a lot of passion and attraction between these strong individuals. Their sexual relations can be a struggle as well as an incredible experience. There will be liberation and warmth and passion. Aquarius will end up respecting Leo if they share true emotions for each other. These two partners will form a very strong connection with each other over time.

If you look at their partnership from a distance, everything will seem simple. However, trust always seems to be a challenge for the two signs. They are both understanding and give each other freedom. But when they are separate from each other, they realize that they know little about their partners and have very little trust in place.

Leo and Aquarius are both heroes. If they fight for the same cause together, they can bring about great change and make a real difference in the world. However, they need to stop fighting with each other if they aim to achieve such things together. If not, their energy will only be scattered in unnecessary fighting.

Aquarius and Virgo

The sexual relationship between the two signs is not easy in any way. They will not be attracted to each other unless there is some strong support in their natal charts. Both signs have natures that will not be supportive of each other. Although Virgo and Aquarius are both intellectuals, they differ greatly from each other. Their tendency to overthink will ruin the possibility of any sexual relationship between the two. The analytical nature of Virgo will be a turnoff for Aquarius, who dislikes overthinking.

Both signs have a rational nature, and this will build trust between them. Virgo usually finds it difficult to trust their partner, but they see no need for this with an Aquarius partner. However, these signs might drift apart even if they have a strong connection at the beginning. For there to be mutual trust, both signs have to be accepting of each other and try to keep their relationship fresh.

Virgo has an adaptable and changeable nature which makes it difficult to accept Aquarius's unchangeable nature. They will be good at communicating with each other and have common topics to discuss. These signs will usually share their interests and be excited about the same things.

Aquarius and Libra

Libra will find it much easier to express themselves sexually when they have an Aquarius partner. The problem with Libra is that they care too much about what other people think. In sexual relations, they will either be too subdued and come across as asexual, or they will try to do too much and make it somewhat awkward for their partner. However, Aquarius is the opposite and does not care about the opinions of others. The sexual relations between the two can be liberating for Libra but challenging for Aquarius, as they have to fight against Libra's need to fit in.

Both signs have a righteous nature, and this will make them trust each other without exception. They have the same insecurities and will help each other overcome them. However, this trust must be built and will not come all at once. These signs like being seen as attractive, and they have to tell each other this. Problems can arise between the two if Libra gets too attached and emotionally dependent on Aquarius. This is something that Aquarius will shy away from.

Both signs have an image to maintain. While Libra likes looking and acting nice towards others, Aquarius is not a crowd-pleaser and likes going the opposite way. Both are stiff in their beliefs and will be unwilling to change their minds.

Aquarius and Scorpio

The sexual relations between Aquarius and Scorpio can be very intense. Together, these signs represent the ultimate sexual freedom with no taboos or restrictions. These air and water signs are very attracted to each other. However, if they break up, they will end up with hateful feelings and despise everything they shared. These signs will find it difficult to balance rational thinking, emotions, and passion. While Scorpio is deeply emotional and has a strong need for sexual relations, Aquarius dislikes too much emotion and has trouble with someone too possessive. Their sex life will either be great or a battleground. Being fixed signs, both will struggle to adapt to a partner very different from them.

Scorpio and Aquarius are straightforward and honest people who should ideally have no problem trusting each other. However, when they get close to each other, this problem will arise: Aquarius will are expected to get tamer and commit to their Scorpio partner. If there is any sign of manipulation in the relationship, things can be out of control. Their partnership will easily break apart because of such things.

Communication is not a problem for these signs if they don't act stubbornly or are too set in their opinions. They can discuss all kinds of strange topics with enjoyment since neither likes making small talk. Small talk seems futile for them both, and they like the fact that they can discuss interesting things with each other. Their connection of depth is incredible, and both have a lot of trouble in understanding many things about society.

Aquarius and Sagittarius

The one important asset for the sexual relations between these signs is that Aquarius tends to act in the way that Sagittarius thinks. They can have a strong attraction towards each other, especially when Sagittarius is at a point where they want confirmation of their sexuality and freedom. The sexual connection between the two can be satisfying, but they are not great when it comes to intimacy. Sagittarius can bring warmth to the relationship, but their focus is easily turned. Both signs understand the need for change in their sex life and will implement it. However, their emotional bond and intimacy are not consistently strong.

Aquarius and Scorpio will understand each other's minds a little too well. Aquarius likes being free, so they can be available to others, while Sagittarius struggles with fidelity. Since both will know this about each other, it will be difficult for them to build trust. They will always question whether they should trust their partner. If they decide to commit to the relationship, they will not be able to give each other the freedom that both need.

If these signs discover a mutual interest, they will never lack subjects to discuss. Their unending discussions could even end up changing their views on a lot of things. Sagittarius is usually a little too talkative while discussing uninteresting topics as they try to connect, and Aquarius can be distant. However, if they find a subject of interest to both, they will share stimulating conversations.

Aquarius and Capricorn

Most people assume that Capricorn is restricting and traditional, while Aquarius is the opposite. In truth, the same planet rules over both signs, which is why they have many similarities. Their different pace is the one problem in their sex life, which is usually due to their different elements. Capricorn is an earth sign that is thorough and slow. They don't jump into a relationship unless they respect their partner and are attracted to them. When they finally indulge in sexual relations, they try to give it their best. As an air sign, Aquarius is a little unreliable and flaky but being ruled by Saturn makes them a lot more reliable than other air signs. They like things to be fast and spontaneous without much overthinking involved. Aquarius will rarely have the patience to deal with Capricorn, who takes time to create a detailed plan. Their need to rush is a turn off for Capricorn. Both signs can be very passionate with the right partner, but these signs are better off as friends than lovers.

Capricorn is set in their convictions and dislikes making any mistakes, while Aquarius values truth and has no fear of confrontation. They both have a different idea of trust, and it is hard for them to accept the differences in their natures. They trust each other but don't have faith that their relationship will work out.

Aquarius and Aquarius

The sexual relationship between two Aquarians can be very interesting and full of excitement. Both will be free in expressing themselves and will also be willing to fulfill each other's fantasies. They follow no restrictions or taboos that society usually dictates. However, the lack of emotional bonding can be an issue for them. This pair will find it difficult to stay together once the initial attraction wears off. They are better suited for occasional flings.

Being from the same sign, they can understand each other without needing words. Freedom will be the foundation of their trust, and neither will want to lie. However, if either becomes too possessive, it will be the end of their relationship.

When two Aquarians have a conversation, it is very difficult for any outsider to actually understand it. They have a great connection when it comes to communication, and ideas are constantly flying around. However, their ego issues will pose a problem.

Aquarius and Pisces

Things will never get boring in the sexual relationship between Aquarius and Pisces. They may not seem like they will initially get along at all, but they can have a great sex life if Pisces avoids getting attached to Aquarius. Pisces will enthusiastically try to maintain an exciting sexual relationship, and Aquarius will follow suit.

Trust can go in two extreme directions for this couple. If they are intimate enough, they will have complete trust with each other. If not, there will be constant suspicion and lies involved. They need to take the time to understand each other if they want to build trust.

Chapter Seven: Aquarius at Work

Aquarians are very capable of many different things, but they are most suited for roles that need unconventional thinking patterns. This sign embodies a lot of professional strengths like assertiveness, social consciousness, and critical thinking. However, they also have their drawbacks, just like any other sign does.

Aquarians lack focus, and they tend to express apathy towards any task that is different from their interests. They always insist on getting their way even if it might not be the right choice while dealing with a particular task. This can have a negative impact on the professional growth of Aquarius despite their better judgment.

However, the positive traits make them great candidates for working in the fields of fine arts, politics, and service. These are some career paths that will help Aquarius flourish in the workplace. It will allow them to work in the way they like while playing on their strengths comfortably.

Aquarians love to display their unique skills, imaginative abilities, intuitive powers, and bold nature. They tend to make conscious efforts to make the world a better place.

They like to display their intellect and talents. They like to exercise these qualities and love to be in an atmosphere where they can propose new ideas and help others by being creative. Creativity and intellectual stimulation drive an Aquarius person. They are good with groups, but they will always strive to be recognized for their personal contributions too.

Aquarius people are humanitarian at heart, so they succeed immensely in occupations that allow them to bring positive changes into the world around them. They are passionate about ideas, knowledge, and new beginnings, so they are great for fields based on discovery and invention such as tech jobs, astronomy, science, etc.

Careers Options for Aquarius Individuals

Mediator

This sign brings deep thinkers who can skillfully think through any problem from an objective standpoint until they find a solution. This is a skill that is important in mediators. Mediators have to remain objective and find practical solutions while keeping a detailed record of any interaction with their clients. Their job is to help two parties communicate more effectively with each other. Mediators may work in a legal setting while helping their clients to document details in their agreement.

Teacher

Since Aquarians have a love for learning, teaching is a great fit for them. If an Aquarian works as a teacher, they can learn a lot more in that specific subject and impart the same knowledge to their students. This sign needs to live in their truth, which makes them more suitable as teachers. Aquarians will always try their best to follow the same rules that they teach their students and thereby set an example for them.

Researcher

As an avid learner and because Aquarians are inquisitive, research is another well-suited field for this sign. Research can be done in teams as well as individually. Researchers have to identify a goal and a certain objective for their research first. After this, they need to create a plan, secure research funding, and finally put their skills to work so they can carry out the project. This is the kind of job that Aquarius will find highly enjoyable and be passionate about. Their inquisitive passion will make them instantly liked by other co-workers on such research projects.

Trainer

Trainers are meant to teach certain skills, standards, or policies to individuals or a group. The assertiveness and critical thinking abilities of Aquarius will help them carry out this task well. They can use it to cleverly instill such knowledge to their students or learners while using their artistic ability to do it in an interesting way.

Actor

Actors have more opportunities than other people to express themselves in different ways. Whether or not it is at a film studio, theatre, or an elaborate set, Aquarius can occupy the spotlight as an actor. They have a very unpredictable nature, and this would make them a delight in improv acting. Their curiosity will also make them work harder at delving into a role and adapting it as their own.

Electrician

The natural curiosity of Aquarius also makes them good at working as an electrician. Their job will be to evaluate electrical failings and provide any potential solutions to their clients. But before they do this, they have to go through all the intricacies of wiring, breakers, and lighting. Playing with these delicate components will be highly enjoyable for Aquarians as they try to get to the core of the problem and then figure out a way to solve it.

Project Manager

As a project manager, Aquarians will have to define a project's objectives, create and implement a budget, and delegate all the tasks to people in the team. This will have to be done to allow the project to be completed more efficiently. Since they are self-isolators, this sign has to put in a little extra effort to be reachable for the team. However, they are great project leaders because they manage to inspire the team even when they are away. Aquarian project managers are great at motivating co-workers to work more fervently.

Scientist

A scientist is always curious, and their curiosity knows no end. This applies to Aquarius individuals as well, and it is why they are naturally suited for the job. They can work in a wide range of fields and decide which area of research they want to focus on. Aquarians will get the chance to gather new information all the time and find answers to all the questions they have.

Environmental Planner

This role's scope is quite vast, which makes the job attractive for Aquarius. Environmental planners usually have to evaluate different lands to determine how they can be used in the best way possible. Their job requires them to collaborate with people from many different professions, which allows them to learn a lot more by asking questions from different professionals and finding answers to their problems. Planners do a lot of research to figure out the advantages and disadvantages involved in using a certain piece of land for a specific purpose. Aquarians will find this job to their liking.

Aquarius in the Workplace

For an Aquarius to feel comfortable at their workplace, their abstract and deep thought process has to be welcomed. This way of thinking comes naturally to them, and if their colleagues and employers appreciate it rather than criticize it, it helps Aquarians grow professionally.

Once they feel at home in their working environment, they will always be willing to help out a colleague or take on someone else's work to lighten their load. This sign loves being helpful to those around them. Their thoughtfulness is a great asset to any workplace. However, this sign comes with some challenges that can also create problems in the workplace. For instance, despite their helpful nature, they are loners. They tend to isolate themselves while working instead of communicating with their team. This is not always acceptable to others, and most colleagues want clear communication from Aquarians.

If Aquarius suddenly goes off-grid without an explanation, it can be a hassle for others at work. To make things easier, the Aquarians should let their co-workers know in advance if they intend to take some solitary time away from work. Being more forthcoming and proactive in communication will make it easier for Aquarius to get along with coworkers. Another challenge that this sign might face is sticking to a schedule. Not all kinds of work can be done at a person's own pace.

Aquarians must overcome their aversion to a fixed routine. They cannot afford to get irritable just because there are deadlines or a schedule to follow. Work is not always aligned according to each individual's personal preferences. This is not a problem that can be fixed, and Aquarians need to learn to deal with it. Work obligations have to be met even if they are boring or difficult at times.

Aquarians usually find it difficult to do any task that is not fulfilling to them or does not bring joy. However, if they focus on the fact that getting the work done on time will give them more free time later, it can be easier for them to work through it. Aquarians will find more enjoyment in their work-life if they reciprocate what they want from work.

Workplace Compatibility with other Zodiac Signs

Aquarius is one of the best signs to have around when you need to hold a brainstorming session. They are original, innovative, and witty. They always come up with some cutting-edge ideas, and they love trying new things. Their vision is admirable and appreciated by all co-workers. However, this sign needs to be careful about who they build a working relationship with. Aquarians focus on the big picture with such intensity they often ignore how others around them feel. These are the kind of things to keep in mind when looking for a working partner. The right sign can make their work-life balance better, while others will only make things more difficult. Reading about the compatibility of Aquarius with other signs at work can be extremely helpful in navigating the professional world.

Aquarius compatibility with other zodiac signs at work:

Aquarius and Aries

The lively partnership between Aries and Aquarius will make work exciting for both signs. Aries is a sign that tends to be a pioneer, while Aquarius is always willing to embark on a new journey. While Aries finds it difficult to stick to a routine, Aquarius doesn't mind dealing with different work responsibilities. Aries has a tendency to take risks, and Aquarius never shied away from signs of danger. They are both similar and compatible in this regard; however, neither is good at dealing with human relations.

Not that they are not sociable; in fact, Aries is quite charming, and Aquarius is a sociable type. However, they both fail to deal well with people they hurt or when confronted by some misunderstanding. These signs need to depend on a third-party water or earth sign who can advise them or take care of any human resource problems.

Aquarius and Taurus

Aquarius and Taurus appear to be complete opposites on the surface. Taurus looks for comfort in familiar things while Aquarius takes a liking to unfamiliar and strange things. Taurus is a grounded sign with their feet on the ground, while Aquarius likes building castles in the air. Taurus tries their best to save money for later while Aquarius has a free hand with spending or giving away money. These differences in their personality make it hard to imagine them working together. However, if they play to their strengths and try mitigating their partner's weaknesses, this can be done. For instance, Aquarius should be the one working on any product development at work while Taurus should be entrusted with financial matters. Aquarius should focus on advertising any services or products at work while Taurus makes their workspace a lot more comfortable to enhance productivity. These signs will work well in industries like recording, real estate development, and retail sales.

Aquarius and Gemini

Aquarius will love working with Gemini colleagues. Both these signs are innovative, witty, and sharp. If they are in the same room, there will be tons of great ideas bouncing off the walls. The one problem with this working pair is that they are not efficient at executing these great ideas. Gemini will always struggle with focusing on a single thing for too long. However, Aquarius can roll their sleeves up to get things done when it is really important. Although Gemini is not very focused, they will still do their bit while Aquarius toils away. Gemini is one of the best types to deal with any last-minute emergencies that would leave others baffled. They are an able and willing sort that Aquarius can depend on. This pair will be successful if they run a business in telecommunications, airlines, or television.

Aquarius and Cancer

Working together will require a lot of compromise from both Cancer and Aquarius. Aquarius is a very logical type, while Cancer is emotional all the time. While Aquarius likes their work environment to be very professional and stark, Cancer wants it to be cozy and familiar. Aquarius likes working with concepts, while Cancer prefers tangible products. If these two signs want to work well together, they have to bridge the gap by drawing on each other's strengths. The leadership skills of Cancer can be helpful for Aquarius. Cancer is great at championing a cause, making long-term plans, and delegating responsibilities in a way that will benefit the workplace. Aquarius is much better at finding innovative solutions for problems that are usually too difficult for others to deal with. These two signs can run a successful business together if they play to their strengths and try making a profession like teaching or catering more interesting.

Aquarius and Leo

Aquarius will find the experience of working with Leo interesting. These two signs are actually the complete opposite of each other. While Leo works just to get the glory, Aquarius likes working for their own satisfaction. While one is more into style, the latter cares about substance. Aquarius is an extremely logical kind, while Leo tends to be too emotional. All these differences make it difficult to imagine that these signs would have a common factor. However, they are both fixed signs, and this means that they look for a secure job. Both generally want constant intellectual stimulation, but they won't seek this at the risk of losing their job. Both signs are also great at working through any difficult projects and making sure they get done to everyone's satisfaction. Their reasons for working hard may be different, but they still get the job done with their incredible stamina. If these signs go into a business together, they should consider a field in film, radio, or television. Aquarius should be the one working on the technical side of things while Leo would be a great performer.

Aquarius and Virgo

Virgo has little common ground with Aquarius. However, there is mutual respect between these two colleagues. Virgo prefers to focus on the little details, while Aquarius is better at looking at the bigger picture. These two co-workers don't allow their emotions to run havoc at the workplace. They stick to their work even if other co-workers go on an ego trip or have a temper tantrum. The methods employed by Virgo can often seem too stuffy for Aquarius. Virgo, on the other hand, finds Aquarius a little inefficient when it comes to working. Despite these differences, their working partnership can be remarkably productive. Some of the most suitable businesses for these two signs to run together are a recycled product store, health food store, or yoga studio. However, if both are employed under someone else, Aquarius should take care of any promotional campaigns while Virgo deals with money matters.

Aquarius and Libra

The work compatibility between Libra and Aquarius is harmonious. When these two signs work together, they have fun even while being productive. While Libra might be a little too clingy for Aquarius at times, their team spirit is admirable. Aquarians should let their Libran partner run free with decorating the workspace. Libra will love to spruce up the space with some pictures, plants, and other things that will allow both to work more comfortably. Most Aquarians don't believe that such things matter when it comes to work and productivity. But once you let your Libra co-worker do this, you realize just how much difference it can make compared to a barren workspace. Both these signs are better at working with concepts than with products. If the business involves scientific research, patents, or intellectual property, these signs will do well. If both signs work under an employer, Libra should be the one dealing with clients while Aquarius handles the authority figures at the office. Aquarius is a lot better at dealing with pushy people and standing their ground. For Libra, this can be too much to handle, and they tend to crumble under pressure.

Aquarius and Scorpio

Both Scorpio and Aquarius are fixed signs. This means that the work dynamic between them can be quite interesting. Both these signs always feel like they are undoubtedly right, and the other person involved is wrong. They have a firm conviction that their work methods are better. Aquarius relies more on cold hard facts, while Scorpio is more emotional. Both signs are gifted in their own way. Aquarius is better at dealing with straightforward things. Scorpio is better able to notice any deception or ferret out a secret. Scorpio should be the one handling any dirty work while Aquarius should handle human-relations matters. It is important for Aquarius to listen to the advice given by their Scorpio colleague or partner since the latter has an uncanny intuition that helps them avoid any scams or fraud. This can be immensely useful for the gullible Aquarius.

Aquarius and Sagittarius

The work compatibility between Sagittarius and Aquarius is actually quite effective. Working together can bring a lot of satisfaction for both signs. Sagittarians admire the innovation, intelligence, and independence of Aquarius. The latter loves the high spirits, humanitarianism, and humor brought by Sagittarius to the workplace. There might be some trouble when Sagittarius starts acting flaky at work because of their lack of focus. However, Aquarians can be insufferably picky about small things like keeping stationery organized or setting the room's temperature. These signs can form a very lucrative partnership if they try to overlook each other's idiosyncrasies. Teaching, Law, or some import-export businesses can be successful ventures for this pair. If both are employees at the same workplace, Aquarians should work on the long-term projects while Sagittarians are better suited for short-term ones. Dividing work in this way will allow both to perform well together.

Aquarius and Capricorn

While Aquarius likes trying new things and changing the old ways, Capricorn is the opposite. However, the old-fashioned Capricorn pairing up with Aquarius is not necessarily a bad idea. Not every old method is outdated or ineffective, and not everything new is productive. If Aquarius can be open to suggestions from their Capricorn colleague, their working relationship can be quite stable. Although Aquarians like shaking things up, they have to admit that a certain security level is necessary for a successful career. Working with a Capricorn can bring this sense of stability. If Aquarians show appreciation for Capricorn's leadership skills, the latter will be a lot easier to work with. They will be much more open to accepting new ideas or innovative strategies from Aquarius at the workplace.

Aquarius and Aquarius

Aquarians are hard to startle, but another member of the same zodiac can manage this. Pairing two people from this zodiac sign together will create a wealth of creativity. The creative capacity of these two colleagues will be endless. Both are interested in cutting-edge technology, and this is why they love working with computers. Radio, telecommunications, and television are possible avenues for a successful career for Aquarius. An Aquarius employee works better alone and should just have only the minimum contact with their employer.

For instance, meeting at the start of the day for a briefing and ending the day with another short meeting is a good option. In the middle, Aquarians should work by themselves to get things done. Both Aquarian colleagues will be independent and can produce great ideas if they are left to work by themselves instead of being forced to work in pairs. Being a fixed sign, the mind of an Aquarius is extremely difficult to change. In any other aspect, this pair can work productively together.

Aquarius and Pisces

Aquarius is usually amused by the quirky techniques Pisces employs at work. Pisces admires the tremendous vision of Aquarius. Although Pisces colleagues can be a little flaky sometimes, Aquarians have their own weaknesses. For instance, Aquarians are not very effusive, and it can be difficult for anyone to understand if they like, hate, or are indifferent towards a project. However, if Aquarians put in a little effort at building a better connection with Pisces colleagues, the latter will work much harder to perform well. If both these signs work under an employer, Aquarius should stick to the analytical aspect of a project while Pisces can deal with any social niceties required at work.

Conclusion

As we come to the end of the book, I would like to thank you for reading it. I hope you found it interesting and useful. There is a lot to learn from the world of astrology and zodiac signs.

By now, you have gained in-depth knowledge about the sign of Aquarius. Each chapter in this book was aimed at providing vital information about the personality of Aquarians and other aspects of their lives.

I hope the information in this guide was helpful in revealing the strengths, weaknesses, and traits of Aquarians. You now know a lot about the best career options suited for people from this sign as well. Learning about the compatibility of Aquarius with other signs will help to navigate relationships with other people.

If used correctly, this book can promote good relationships between an Aquarius and people from other zodiac signs. It will also help Aquarians understand themselves better and improve mental, physical, spiritual, and financial wellbeing. Thank you again for making it to the end. Please recommend it to any friends or family who might benefit from the book as well.

Here's another book by Mari Silva that you might like

Your Free Gift (only available for a limited time)

Thanks for getting this book! If you want to learn more about various spirituality topics, then join Mari Silva's community and get a free guided meditation MP3 for awakening your third eye. This guided meditation mp3 is designed to open and strengthen ones third eye so you can experience a higher state of consciousness. Simply visit the link below the image to get started.

https://spiritualityspot.com/meditation

References

8 Things to Know About Your Aquarius Child. (n.d.). www.mom365.com website: https://www.mom365.com/mom/astrology/all-about-your-aquarius-childs-astrology

Aquarius Friendship Compatibility. (2020, October 7). Tarot.com website: https://www.tarot.com/astrology/compatibility/friends/aquarius

Aquarius relationships. (n.d.). website: https://www.compatible-astrology.com/aquarius-relationships.html

Aquarius-Pisces Cusp. (n.d.). astrologyk.com website: http://astrologyk.com/zodiac/cusp/aquarius-pisces

A, J. (2020, January 30). 5 Aquarius Celebrities Who Are Exactly Like Their Zodiac Sign (& 5 Who Aren't). TheTalko website: https://www.thetalko.com/aquarius-celebrities-fit-dont-fit-zodiac-sign/

Birthstone for Aquarius Zodiac Sign: Lucky Birthstone for 21st and about February 20th. (2019, February 1). Gemstone Blog, Diamond Article, Jewelry News, Gemology Online website: https://shubhgems.com/blog/birthstone-for-aquarius-zodiac-sign

Characteristics of Capricorn-Aquarius Cusps You Never Knew About. (2015, January 30). Astrology Bay website: https://astrologybay.com/capricorn-aquarius-cusp-characteristics

Definition of Every Zodiac Cusp Sign & Dates | Astrology.com. (n.d.). www.astrology.com website: https://www.astrology.com/on-the-cusp

Denise. (2018, April 21). The Aquarius Man: Key Traits In Love, Career, And Life. i.TheHoroscope.co website: https://i.thehoroscope.co/the-aquarius-man-key-traits-in-love-career-and-life/

Denise. (2018, April 28). The Aquarius Woman: Key Traits In Love, Career, And Life. i.TheHoroscope.co website: https://i.thehoroscope.co/the-aquarius-woman-key-traits-in-love-career-and-life/

Denise. (2018, November 12). Aquarius Qualities, Positive and Negative Traits. i.TheHoroscope.co website: https://i.thehoroscope.co/aquarius-qualities-positive-and-negative-traits/

Denise. (2018, November 11). Aquarius Weaknesses: Know Them so You Can Defeat Them. i.TheHoroscope.co website: https://i.thehoroscope.co/aquarius-weaknesses-know-them-so-you-can-defeat-them/

Denise. (2018, April 21). The Aquarius Child: What You Must Know About This Little Trendsetter. i.TheHoroscope.co website: https://i.thehoroscope.co/the-aquarius-child-what-you-must-know-about-this-little-trendsetter/

Green, I. (2018, October 29). The Aquarius Sign: A Deep Analysis of Aquarian Signs and Symbols. Trusted Psychic Mediums website: https://trustedpsychicmediums.com/aquarius-star-sign/aquarius-symbol/

Hall, M. (2019, March 20). What's the Meaning of the 11th House in Astrology? LiveAbout website: https://www.liveabout.com/the-eleventh-house-207252

Ingle, P. (2020, January 10). 10 Things That You Should Know About an Aquarius Child. parenting.firstcry.com website: https://parenting.firstcry.com/articles/10-things-that-you-should-know-about-an-aquarius-child/

Lawrence, A. (2020, July 23). Dating an Aquarius: What to Expect - PairedLife - Relationships. pairedlife.com website: https://pairedlife.com/compatibility/Dating-an-Aquarius-What-to-Expect

Leal, S. (2019, July 31). Here's Your Power Color, Based on Your Astrological Sign. Apartment Therapy website: https://www.apartmenttherapy.com/this-is-your-color-power-according-to-your-astrological-sign-36629958

Learn About Every Zodiac Cusp Sign and Dates! (2020, May 9). Medium website: https://medium.com/@meraastro.com/learn-about-every-zodiac-cusp-sign-and-dates-bad106c7d5f3

Love advice for Aquarius people. (2019, December 7). www.timesnownews.com website: https://www.timesnownews.com/astrology/aquarius-horoscope/article/love-advice-for-aquarius-people/524042

Muniz, H. (2020, January 2). The 7 Aquarius Traits You Need to Know. blog.prepscholar.com website: https://blog.prepscholar.com/aquarius-traits-personality

My Aquarius Zodiac Sign: Parent & Child. (n.d.). www.horoscope.com website: https://www.horoscope.com/zodiac-signs/aquarius/parent-child

My Aquarius Zodiac Sign: Friendship. (n.d.). www.horoscope.com website: https://www.horoscope.com/zodiac-signs/aquarius/friendship

Rubino, S. (2020, August 12). 6 Skills You Should Master This Summer. Thrillist website: https://www.thrillist.com/lifestyle/nation/6-skills-you-should-master-this-summer

Robinson, A. (2020, March 17). Aquarius Compatibility: Which Sign Is the Best Match? blog.prepscholar.com website: https://blog.prepscholar.com/aquarius-compatibility-signs

White, E. (2018, September 27). Aquarius Child: Personality Traits and Characteristics | Aquarius Baby. ZodiacSigns-Horoscope.com website: https://www.zodiacsigns-horoscope.com/aquarius/aquarius-child-personality-traits/

Printed in Great Britain
by Amazon